CHURCH LABYRINTHS

Questions & answers regarding the history, relevance, and use of labyrinths in churches

©

2001 by Robert Ferré

Revised edition: 2013

Labyrinth Enterprises, LLC
www.labyrinth-enterprises.com

INTRODUCTION TO REVISED EDITION

It seems impossible that I first wrote this book a dozen years ago. At that time, I was in my sixth year as a full time labyrinth maker. Back then, when I gave lectures or did research, there were only a few resources available. (I had just co-edited the English translation of the Hermann Kern labyrinth compendium, *Through the Labyrinth: Designs and Meanings Over 5,000 Years*.) Now, labyrinth books are plentiful. I have more than 100 in my personal library.

Nevertheless, I feel a simple and direct book on this topic may still be well received. I have expanded it by adding material from my website, www.labyrinth-enterprises.com, namely, 12 reasons why a church should have a labyrinth.

I originally wrote this book to present the labyrinth in church acceptable language. I avoid non-Christian language and traditions but for a brief mention. This was meant to make the book acceptable to conservative boards of trustees. But more than that, it reflects the fact that there is a verifiable and long established Christian labyrinth tradition, almost as old as the church itself.

There is no particular organization to the question and answer format. It has the feeling of an interview which hops from here to there without a pattern. In editing the early edition, I am surprised at how few changes need to be made. I still hold most of these opinions and reflect them in current writing.

It is my intention to make my early books, now out of print, available, whether on my website (www.labyrinth-enterprises.com), on electronic media, or using publish on demand services. In addition, I am working on my larger three-volume opus, comprising the ultimate construction manual, guidelines for facilitators and a collection of essays (still years from completion). The availability of my upcoming writing should be heralded on my website and in various social media.

As always, I invite your feedback, corrections, and suggestions. I can be contacted at this email: robert@labyrinth-enterprises.com. Thank you for your interest in labyrinths.

CHURCH LABYRINTHS

Robert, what led you to the labyrinth?

I became involved with labyrinths because of my long-time affinity for Chartres Cathedral in France. During the last 48 years I have visited Chartres 53 times, including leading groups there on pilgrimage for 17 years. In February of 1995 I read an article about a woman in California who was using the Chartres labyrinth in her church. That caught my attention. She was the Reverend Dr. Lauren Artress, a psychotherapist and an Episcopal priest (canon) at Grace Cathedral in San Francisco. Had she been using a labyrinth from anywhere but Chartres Cathedral, it may never have grabbed my attention. Chartres was the key factor. That article led me to study – and to eventually make – labyrinths.

Was Dr. Artress the first to rediscover the labyrinth?

No, but for churches, she's been a leading influence. Rev. Artress headed a program called Quest, which was investigating new, meaningful ways to bring spirituality into modern life. After she discovered the labyrinth at a Jean Houston mystery school event, she noted that people responded very favorably to it. I find it a bit ironic that one of the best solutions to finding a progressive ministry for the church turned out not to be something new and revolutionary, but rather, utilizing an ancient tool which had been lying dormant since the Middle Ages. Artrress subsequently founded Veriditas, a non-profit organization that offers programs and labyrinth facilitator training (see www.veriditas.org).

What are the origins of the labyrinth?

Labyrinths go back at least 5,000 years, long before Christianity. The oldest examples are found in petroglyphs found in Galicia, Spain, and Goa, India. Of course spirals and circles are even older, but I'm referring to patterns with a unicursal design, having a single path that leads to the center. Some conservative churches have expressed a concern that the labyrinth might be a pagan device of some kind. The church has adopted many pagan practices, changing them for specific Christian use (Christmas and Easter, for example). Similarly, the labyrinth was given a new context, symbolism and meaning. As a result, church labyrinths have developed a specifically Christian tradition that dates from the early Middle Ages.

How was the labyrinth changed for Christian use?

The labyrinth pattern evolved from the classic 7-circuit labyrinth (below, left) into its medieval form, which reached the highest and most elegant form in Chartres Cathedral at the beginning of the 13th century (below, right). The process began in the fourth century when, 11 years after Constantine made Christianity legal, a Roman mosaic labyrinth was placed into a church in North Africa and Christianized by adding the words *"sancta eclesia"* (holy church) in

the center. A few centuries later, labyrinth drawings began to show up in the margins and blank pages of manuscripts. The first step was to make the labyrinth circular, as a circle has only one center (God) and its perimeter is continuous (eternity). Then, the number of paths was increased to eleven, and finally, internal turns added which give the labyrinth a cruciform appearance. This process was completed by the eighth century. Ultimately, in Chartres, the central petals and perimeter lunations were added, along with specific numerical proportions known as sacred geometry. For more details on the origins of this pattern, see my book *Origin, Symbolism, and Design of the Chartres Labyrinth*.

So there are both Christian and non-Christian labyrinths?

There are a number of traditions which use the labyrinth, one of which is Christian. The classic 7-circuit labyrinth is far more widespread than the Chartres labyrinth, partly due to the simplicity of its pattern. It is found all over the world. When people make labyrinths in their backyard, even to use for Christian purposes, many times it is the classic 7-circuit design. I think the distinction between Christian and non-Christian labyrinths is getting rather vague. Medieval labyrinths were indoors, inside the cathedrals, whereas classic labyrinths were largely outdoors, in nature. Now, there are many outdoor Chartres labyrinths, including one at the Unitarian Universalist church in Elgin, Illinois, which is called the Earth Wisdom labyrinth. Other labyrinths, being used generically for spiritual practice, are not associated with any specific church or denomination. The labyrinth is a blank slate that can be used for any tradition, or none at all.

Are labyrinths used in both Catholic and Protestant settings?

Yes. In the beginning, since Dr. Artress is an Episcopal priest, many of her first events were within that denomination. However, she soon began presenting the labyrinth not only to other denominations, but also within secular contexts for psychologists and women's groups. Since the labyrinth originated in Gothic cathedrals, most Catholic groups have readily accepted it. We have made labyrinths for a number of convents and retreat centers as well as churches of all descriptions and denominations (including Baptist). Several favorable articles in Methodist newsletters spurred an interest there. We have also installed a labyrinth for a synagogue, and know of a Buddhist retreat center with a labyrinth. I believe all of this reflects the universal appeal of the labyrinth, and its potential use in many situations and circumstances. This book is specifically about church labyrinths, but of course they exist in schools, public parks, private homes, and many other places.

So the use of labyrinths is now quite diverse?

Yes. I think people are using the labyrinth to introduce a spiritual, inner experience within secular settings. For example, we have placed labyrinths in hospitals, where it can compliment the outer healing that science offers by accessing a means to find inner healing. At VA hospitals, the labyrinth represents safe ground, whereas in Iraq the ground blew up and took their legs with it. Labyrinths cross virtually all cultural settings, often used in generic ways for well being, diversion, play, and stress reduction.

What sets apart the use of labyrinths in churches?

Just as the church must find its appropriate context and identity in the world at large, so must it decide on how it can best use labyrinths. I came across materials from a group in England that designed their own labyrinth pattern with numerous openings along the path. They call it "The Prayer Path: A Christ-Centered Labyrinth Experience." It incorporates multi-media, such as computer monitors, videos, and music. In the 11 openings the participants engage in a series of processes designed to open to prayer, release hurts, explore relationships, find their place in the world, etc. A labyrinth of any design can be used for similar purposes, for examining our relationship with God and the world around us. Some churches have added stations of the cross. Mostly, churches use the labyrinth as a means for walking prayer, meditation and focussed attention.

Can one combine pagan and Christian labyrinth traditions?

Sometimes, but I don't think it's a very good fit. Mixing traditions can lead to misunderstanding. When Dr. Artress gave a keynote address at a national labyrinth conference, her suggestion was, "Know your audience and explain the labyrinth in their language." As a labyrinth maker, I am often asked about the correct orientation of the labyrinth – which direction it should face. There are two answers, one Christian, one not. Gothic cathedrals had a very specific orientation, with the entrance to the west. You enter facing east, the direction of the rising sun (symbolizing the risen Son, hope, new birth). In other traditions, it is common to use dowsing as a means for asking the earth itself what the orientation of the labyrinth should be, based on assumptions of devic or earth energies that may not be comfortable for some churches. While many churches use the labyrinth generically, in a neutral way, very few actually adopt pagan practices. (I once told a Universalist Unitarian church that the classic labyrinth pattern they had chosen has specifically pagan associations, to which they replied, "Great! That's just what we want.")

What is the connection between dowsing and labyrinths?

Many people picture dowsers as holding a forked stick, looking for water sources. That's one use, but there's more than that. Dowsing is another way to tap into the great Wisdom that is out there, available to any of us when we are quiet or sensitive enough. The dowsing community began using labyrinths at their national and regional gatherings as far back as the mid-1980's—predating the church revival. Besides determining the specifics regarding the labyrinth (size, location, orientation, etc.), one dowser I know begins by asking the local spirits if he has their permission to install a labyrinth there, lest he upset them. I wonder if they have ever said "no."

Is dowsing to be avoided?

Dowsing is an alternative tradition based on different principles. Like the labyrinth, it is a spiritual tool. For dowsers, the power of the labyrinth comes from the earth, and the mechanics of how it is set up. One morning, in Chartres Cathedral, I discovered a man lying in the center of the labyrinth, presumably hoping to gain some energy there from. Like dowsers, he apparently believed that power comes from the labyrinth itself. Such an approach is not consistent

9

with the way most churches use labyrinths. (It also irks the clergy in Chartres Cathedral.)

Do any churches use dowsing?

I know of some that have. In my mind, the medieval church had a lot more rapport with nature than we do today. Since God created the earth, they felt it was suitable to interact with nature without identifying it as pagan. Perhaps they even used dowsing. I have seen dowsing used appropriately within a church setting. In one instance, dowsing was used to locate unmarked graves in a cemetery prior to installing a new road. During the construction, they didn't disturb a single grave. I see no problem with using all spiritual tools if they serve their intended purpose.

Where does the church feel the power of the labyrinth originates?

For the most part, the church tradition holds that the power of the labyrinth comes not from the earth or the proper location of the labyrinth, but from the act of walking it. When one is on pilgrimage, the power comes from the inner experience, not from the road itself. It comes from the walking, not the route. It coes from the experience, not the labyrinth itself. That being said, the nature of the road and the route (and the labyrinth) can still play an important role in pilgrimage. Walking up a steep mountain differs considerably from walking through the desert. The best labyrinths don't draw attention to themselves, serving just as a guided path for us to follow.

How does generic use differ from Christian use?

The labyrinth is very effective as a generic, non-dogmatic means for meditation and well being. It can be used in establishing equilibrium, problem solving, or enhancing one's creativity or intuition. It lends itself well to a number of rituals and ceremonies. These can be done in either a Christian or a non-religious fashion. Sometimes the difference is only a semantic one. Generically, I might say that I am using the labyrinth for meditation, or that it leads me to my Higher Self. Within a Christian context, I would say that I am using the labyrinth as a form of body prayer, or walking prayer, and that it is leading me to God. I think exactly the same thing is happening, just the syntax is different. Many of the generic uses are in fact very spiritual. Basically, "spirituality" is a generic term whereas "religion" or "Christianity" imply a more specific focus on form or theology. Some people feel there is more room for them in the generic version. If that's true, the church needs to do a better job in presenting itself.

So churches have a narrower use of the labyrinth?

Usually, and appropriately so. One author suggests that the labyrinth could cause harm by turning the church generic, thereby losing its specific Christian identity in favor of a more vague, vanilla, generalized spirituality. I think loss of identity is a real concern. That's what Chartres Cathedral has been facing, as it seeks to accommodate the burgeoning interest in the labyrinth (and tourism in general) within its mission as a working, parish church. Where does it draw the line of acceptability? Is it necessary to discard 2,000 years of tradition? Hopefully not.

Aren't churches becoming more generic?

I believe the statistics show that the interest in spirituality is growing rapidly, but the growth of churches doesn't correspond. It might be that churches can't hold on to narrow views any more if they want to have a wide appeal. Many seekers look askance on institutions that claim to posses the *only* path to salvation. But if there are many paths, what criteria do people have for choosing one over another? This is a dilemma for all churches. Perhaps having a labyrinth can make one church more unique or "competitive" or accessible than another. I have seen churches buy labyrinths especially to offer a broader, more generic attraction, to give people a spiritual practice within the church, hoping that once drawn into the fold, they will become active in the church's mission in other ways as well. Will the labyrinth rescue dying churches? Probably not. Certainly churches can't be all things to all people. Perhaps the labyrinth itself will lead us to the answer, to a middle ground.

Is there in fact an identifiable Christian labyrinth tradition?

Sister Anne Marie, a nun living in Chartres (now retired), used to give three labyrinth walks per year in what she said was the "traditional" way. Groups walked in procession, together, at the same speed, in single file, into the labyrinth, to the center, then out the top of the labyrinth, up the aisle to the altar, which was the final destination. I don't know to what tradition she was referring, or how she learned it. As far as actual use and practices, there are no contemporary written records from the Middle Ages describing their use of labyrinths except for one account of cathedral priests (canons) doing a dance on the labyrinth at Easter time in Auxerre Cathedral.

Do we know any details of the canon's labyrinth dance?

We know that they passed a ball back and forth between the Dean and the canons, but few other details. In the fourteenth century, the cathedral chapter in Chartres passed a rule forbidding parishioners from dancing on the labyrinth, which leads to the obvious conclusion that they must have been dancing. PErhaps the church felt it was appropriate only for the clergy.

Why was the labyrinth included in Gothic churches?

We have to use logic and historical context to uncover the purpose of labyrinths. Located in the nave, from pillar to pillar, it's hard to imagine that the labyrinth was not intended for public walking. You can't avoid it except by detouring through the side aisles. It reflects and symbolizes, as does every other part of the cathedral, the journey from this world to the next, from earth to heaven. In other words, salvation. Certain ideas gain favor and get repeated over and over—for example, that the labyrinth was designated as a substitute form of pilgrimage when it was too dangerous to go to the Holy

Land. Perhaps, but there is no historical record of it. Such theories are just conjecture.

And of course, it can be used for prayer.

Yes, of course. That is always appropriate. For people who don't sit still very easily for long periods of time, the labyrinth occupies their bodies while their minds go deeply into prayer. It enhances the process. I once saw a slogan by a dance company that said, "move the body, free the mind." Labyrinths move the body while calming the mind, an excellent state for prayer.

Doesn't the labyrinth do more than just keep the body busy?

Oh, yes, much more. Besides the physical phenomenon, such as balancing the hemispheres of the brain, I believe the labyrinth helps to organize our experience. For example, I sometimes make temporary labyrinths out of rope. Before I arrive, the site is just a park or the front yard of a church. With the rope in place, people walk in a special, concentrated way, often having meaningful experiences. When we're finished, I pull up the rope and once more it is just a patch of grass, as it was before. But for those two hours, it was something different. Walking in a certain pattern for a certain purpose doesn't just distract the body; it produces something tangible.

Couldn't the same thing happen just walking around the block?

Theoretically, but probably not. Walking the labyrinth involves more than just focus and concentration. I believe a logos is created which is like a spirit or energy that is greater than the sum of the parts (people walking). Plus, the geometry has a specific effect, especially when the labyrinth is circular. We are by nature circular, our atoms, our DNA, the movement of the planets. St. Augustine is often quoted by labyrinth people because of his phrase, *"Solvitur ambulando" (It is solved by walking).* That relates to a piece of advice that I received years ago regarding spiritual guidance: Sometimes the answer isn't ready, or the circumstances aren't right to receive it. The instructions were to ask, but don't be anxious or impatient as to when (or for that matter, how) the answer may come. That's how a labyrinth works. Be patient. Just walk, being attentive and open and willing. The effect of labyrinth walking is cumulative. Perhaps you will not notice a result until you have walked it more than once, or a dozen times, or a hundred. It's not difficult; most people can do it. That's why the labyrinth is so accessible.

Do people appreciate how ancient the labyrinth is?

Not always. Several times I have spoken about labyrinths to ninth graders at a local middle school. Thinking about how the labyrinth would be relevant for them, I realized that their entire life is based around modern phenomena, from hanging out at the mall to using computers and cell phones. They do very little, if anything, that connects them to the past, to their ancestors, to ancient rituals, to anything before the 21st century. But when they are walking a labyrinth, they are following the footsteps of millions of labyrinth walkers over thousands of years who have done exactly the same thing. The labyrinth is like a bridge between the past and the present. As such, I believe it takes us beyond ourselves, to the bigger picture, and even to Truth itself.

We find Truth in the labyrinth? Do you mean God?

Jesuit paleontologist Pierre Teillard de Chardin wrote about a phenomenon he called the Omega Point. When seeking for truth, which is a spiritual quest, we don't look out in the world of illusion where it can't be found. Rather, we go within, through prayer and contemplation and creativity. We find truth by being very specific, by personalizing the quest. Once we find it, we realize Truth applies universally to everything. So we go inside individually, but when we reach the Omega Point, we find All That Is. Thus, that which is the most personal is also the most universal. When we walk a labyrinth, we go not only to the center of the labyrinth, but to the center of ourselves. Granted, some people fear that if we go inside we will find a horrible cesspool of sin and depravity. On an airplane, I met a woman whose religious beliefs forbade meditation, because she was taught that if you quiet your mind, the devil will take possession of it. I don't think so. I believe that we are made in God's image. To find our true and authentic self is a spiritual and healing experience. It is indeed finding God. Labyrinths are a great help in this process. They serve as a gateway to the invisible world of spirit.

So, walking a labyrinth isn't a selfish act?

Every great spiritual teacher first went through a time of self-development, of enlightenment, after which he or she was then equipped to help others. Dealing with vague generalities won't do. We need deep personal experience first in order to effectively help others.

Do people walk the labyrinth alone, then?

The United States is the land of individualism carried to the extreme. When we hold labyrinth walks, people have commented that they were initially distressed by the size of the group, as they usually prefer to walk the labyrinth alone. They feel other walkers will get in their way, disturb their experience. What they find, however, surprises them. The act of walking together in community actually strengthens the experience. It reminds them that we are all on the same path, going to the same goal, even though it may appear to be chaos. In the same way, I find that meditating with a large group is very powerful. It helps me go deeper. It inspires me. The labyrinth can be walked alone or in groups. Each have their particular benefit.

Do most people respond in the same way to walking the labyrinth?

There are some commonalities. People quickly grasp that the labyrinth is a metaphor for life. In life there are many twists and turns. We think we have reached dead ends, or gotten off the track, but in fact, we are just changing direction. We're not wasting our time. As in life, there are limitless possibilities and levels of experience on the labyrinth. It meets each of us where we are and helps take us to the next level, the next stage in our spiritual unfolding. That process varies for each person. Therefore, we always emphasize that there is nothing that is *supposed* to happen when walking a labyrinth. The visual picture is misleading, as it seems that everyone is doing the same thing. In reality, there are differences in pace, timing, footwork, intent, and experience. One woman said that nothing had happened during her labyrinth walk, except that she felt a pervasive sense of peace. That's not nothing!

How does the labyrinth work?

I see the labyrinth as a magnifier. Whatever happens to us in life, happens to us in the labyrinth, much like the zen principle that states "how we do anything is how we do everything." In the sharing session following a labyrinth walk, someone will tell how she inadvertently missed a turn and found herself back at the entrance, having never reached the center. Then she realizes that in life, she often starts out on a project, only to be thwarted and to never reach completion, never arrive at her goal. Her labyrinth experience reflected her life. By making her pattern evident, the labyrinth facilitated that insight. The same is true in how people walk the labyrinth itself, whether they go fast or slow, how they accommodate other people they encounter on the path. I never specify how people should walk the labyrinth. I let them find their own comfort level.

So the labyrinth is like a mirror?

Yes, the labyrinth helps us to see ourselves more clearly. People often have revelations and insights on the labyrinth. This is possible because the labyrinth bypasses the rational mind. There are no intersections, no alternate routes to puzzle over, no decisions to be made. The labyrinth serves as "time out" for our intellect. It can take a break. That's helpful, because the intellect is a huge barrier. Bypassing it, we get beyond the surface operation of our mind, into deeper territory. Modern life is lived almost completely on the surface, engaged largely in appearances. The labyrinth moves people so deeply because it takes them to new territory and important discoveries about themselves.

The intellect takes a break?

Every spiritual tradition has some technique or process to achieve this purpose. Eastern traditions call intellectual activity the "monkey mind," which jumps from thought to thought like a monkey in the trees. Much of our society operates only on that level, which is very shallow. By going deeper, beyond that, the labyrinth takes us to new territory. In spiritual terms, it takes us away from our egos and towards God. Sometimes people can't describe in words what they feel, but they know something important happened. That's why after a labyrinth walk we often supply art materials for people to draw as a nonintellectual response to their experience. We can't think our way to enlightenment. That's why science will never be successful in determining the effectiveness of labyrinths. Science operates in a different realm and speaks a different language.

Is there much written about labyrinths?

The "bible" for the use of labyrinths in churches in *Walking a Sacred Path: Rediscovering the Labyrinth as a Spiritual Tool* by the Reverend Dr. Lauren Artress, a canon at Grace Cathedral in San Francisco. Very articulate, she has been very focused in using the labyrinth in a Christian way. Scores of books have been written about the labyrinth. The greatest compendium on labyrinths was written by Hermann Kern and published in German in 1982 and in English in 2000. Kern is highly opinionated but he has an amazing amount of history and detail in a single volume. Alas, it went out of print. If you ever see a used copy of *Through the Labyrinth* for under one hundred dollars, snatch it up. Jill Kimberly Hartwell Geoffrion has written numerous mystical books about the labyrinth and Chartres Cathedral. Perhaps the most articulate expression of the relevance of labyrinths in churches is *Labyrinths From the Outside In*, by Donna Schaper and Carol Ann Camp. At the end of this volume are quotations from some of these and other books.

In Chartres they don't use their labyrinth?

No. When you ask people who have lived in Chartres all their lives whether they have ever walked the labyrinth, they almost always say no. They go to church, attend mass, and go home. The labyrinth has not been presented as a part of everyday spiritual practice. As a result, the administration doesn't support what it calls "labyrinth tourism." I find that strange. Do they object to stained glass window tourism? Architectural tourism? I once organized a labyrinth walk in the cathedral after closing hours to which I invited local acquaintances—about 20 or so. Adults, life long residents of Chartres, most had never walked the labyrinth before. The labyrinth is generally uncovered on Fridays, except for special occasions and construction. Best to check in advance.

Is America leading the revival in the use of labyrinths?

Probably, in sheer numbers, but we don't have a monopoly on the labyrinth. The labyrinth revival has taken place predominantly in English and German speaking countries, as well as some popularity in Holland. I would say, however, that within churches, the revival is much stronger in the United States than elsewhere. Jill Geoffrion has a ministry which takes labyrinths to Third World countries, such as the People's Republic of Congo and Myanmar. She finds they are very well received and utilized. See her website, www.jillgeoffrion.com, which also has excellent material and photos of Chartres Cathedral, as well as her personal blog, which is found at www.throughjillseyes.wordpress.com.

Are labyrinths a fad?

We are now 30 years into the revival movement, which is still going strong. Is that a fad? Probably not. A fad usually consists of something new, but in fact, we are reviving something old, something proven. That's different. That's why so many writers refer to the labyrinth as an archetype, because it keeps appearing and reappearing in human experience. Far from being a fad, I think the labyrinth has appeared periodically throughout history at times of spiritual turmoil. Our modern times are so far out of balance that a tool is needed that can help restore equilibrium. The labyrinth has answered the call.

How many churches have labyrinths?

Thousands. And personal labyrinths outnumber church labyrinths by a factor of two or three. Some effort has been made to locate and quantify the labyrinths in the world, especially the website www.labyrinthlocator.com. It is a joint effort between Veriditas and The Labyrinth Society. Labyrinths are listed only if someone uploads the information. That means the website is substantially incomplete. Still, there are several thousand listed there, with locations all around the world. If you are traveling and want to see if there are labyrinths in a particular locality, go to the website and conduct a search. If you are the caretaker of a labyrinth, be sure to list it there.

How do churches organize the use of their labyrinths?

Typically, there is a labyrinth committee, which is trained in the history and use of the labyrinth. In the case of portable labyrinths, some churches set up a regular schedule for access by the public, such as once a week or twice a month. Many find that due to popularity, they subsequently increase the frequency of the labyrinth walks. Often there are candles and soft music. I know that some churches use labyrinths with groups such as AA. Most make the labyrinths open to the public. Volunteers perform any landscaping and maintenance duties.

Are some labyrinths open 24 hours a day?

Yes. After having a portable labyrinth, many churches look into making a permanent outdoor labyrinth that is open day and night. Usually there are benches for sitting, perhaps lighting and other amenities. I installed a labyrinth in St. Louis, Missouri, in front of a downtown church, which regards it as community outreach. The minister reports that every day at 6:00 p.m. they see the same man, dressed in a suit and carrying a briefcase, walking the labyrinth, apparently unwinding on his way home from work. It is estimated that over a million people have walked the labyrinth on the terrace outside of Grace Cathedral in San Francisco. At this writing, in 2013, the steps and terrace are being redone. When and if the labyrinth will be replaced is uncertain.

Is there no assurance how public labyrinths will be used?

No. In a democracy, you have to accept the possibility of fringe elements. Grace Cathedral reports an incident in which a man showed up wearing full pagan regalia, including a headdress with antlers. These kinds of things make churches a bit nervous. Labyrinths are indeed a public service and should properly be located in public spaces, schools, hospitals, airports – everywhere. In Chartres, access to the labyrinth is restricted partly because of their concern of its misuse. Labyrinths in ancient times may have been used only by the properly initiated, and then removed. Now we put them in public places hoping that people of all types and beliefs will discover and use them.

Are youth attracted to labyrinths?

Twice I have installed labyrinths for large national conferences of church youth (one Catholic, one Lutheran). The organizers of the conferences were surprised by how the youth took to the labyrinth. At the Lutheran conference, I was called back to make a second labyrinth to handle the demand. We also rented labyrinths numerous ties to church youth organizations.

What happened to the labyrinths in Gothic cathedrals?

Most were removed during the 18th century, which identified itself as the "Age of Enlightenment." Religion in general was in disfavor, replaced by science and rational thinking. Great destruction was also done to cathedrals and churches themselves. In several of them, stained glass windows were destroyed to let in more light, so that the clergy could be better seen. Some renowned buildings were dynamited and the stone sold. The word "Gothic" itself was pejorative, meaning barbarian, like the Goths who overran Rome. The ages of reason and enlightenment were busy splitting apart body and mind and spirit. They were dedicated to scientific thinking and discovery. Earlier, when the Gothic cathedrals were built, God was the measure of all things. By the eighteenth century, man held himself as the measure of all things. God was pushed out. They couldn't understand why anyone would walk in circles, as they wanted to be linear, rational, efficient. In the 19th century, the great cathedrals came to be appreciated again, but most of the labyrinths were already gone.

Are we more enlightened now?

Our perception of ourselves and the world resembles that of the eighteenth century far more than that of the twelfth and thirteenth centuries. Although quantum physics has disproved the Newtonian idea that the universe is mechanical, like a clock, which we can enslave for our own purposes, such an attitude is still very prevalent today. Every culture makes its temples the tallest and most visible structures. In the Middle Ages, it was cathedrals. These days, banks and office buildings tower over our cities. These reveal our actual religion: commerce. How enlightened is that?

How can we learn from the Middle Ages?

One way is to study what they did, their art, their sacred geometry. Chartres Cathedral is like an encyclopedia, like a sermon in glass and stone. I think there is much to be learned there. In a movement known as Scholasticism, schools such as the one at Chartres were rediscovering the great thinkers of antiquity. One of the great teachers, Bernard of Chartres, said that if we can see further than those who came before us, it is only because we midgets are standing on the shoulders of giants. Without them, we would be nothing. It is a great mistake to overrate ourselves, or think those who came before us were ignorant (as they did in the eighteenth century). One of my favorite statements about Chartres Cathedral, from geometer Michael Schneider, says that it may be a mystery, but it is no secret. It is available to any of us to learn from it.

What led to the construction of Gothic cathedrals?

That's a huge topic, to which many scholarly books have been dedicated. One thing is sure, you don't completely change your architecture and begin to build towering cathedrals without such a movement being supported by an enormous public vision and energy. The era during which Gothic cathedrals emerged was a time of great growth, hope, discovery, and prosperity. The weather improved; political stability led to peace. Previous churches had been built like fortresses, whereas Gothic churches, with walls of glass, can't be defended. They reflect a new openness, when cities began to grow, mobility increased, inventions made life easier, and guilds and trades led to the rise of the middle class. One author suggests that only when people were able to conceive of such glorious buildings were they then able to invent the technologies necessary to do it.

Where did the knowledge come from to build Gothic cathedrals?

Throughout the area north of Paris, over a period of 150 years, builders experimented and invented techniques. I think of these as individual instruments. Then in Chartres Cathedral, for the first time, the entire symphony played. All the bits and pieces of knowledge were assembled in a way that became the model for all subsequent Gothic churches. In some ways the masons were conservative, as with the massive buttresses. Yet in other ways, they were audacious in what they attempted, and accomplished. The true story is so much more inspiring than the hokey so-call mysteries involving Templars and buried treasures. They overcame the limitations of stone in ways never discovered by the Romans or Egyptians or Mayans. The answer lay in having the parts all work together, in dynamic tension, rather than just piling up stones. But that's another book.

Can you say more about the school in Chartres?

Absolutely. Chartres was a place of great intellectual inquiry. It was one of the most recognized centers of learning in the Middle Ages. Geometry, mathematics, astronomy, and other topics (the seven liberal arts) were taught there. The twelfth century was like a mini-Renaissance but with one difference. The talent and knowledge and learning were informed by religious intent and devotion, often dedicated to the Virgin Mary. The school faded from significance after the founding of secular universities.

What can we learn from Gothic cathedrals?

Scholars tell us that medieval theological principles were expressed in artistic form – in sculpture, stained glass, and the architecture itself. This was an era in which salvation was still foremost in people's minds. That's why labyrinths were placed in the center of the nave, where they couldn't be missed. They, along with the windows, the sculptures, and the entire architecture, represent the path to salvation, from this world to the next, from the mundane to the spiritual. Cathedrals sharpen our focus on God. In the face of such determination and magnificence, we are inspired and challenged to look at our own values and to what end we are using our own talents.

Are there erroneous theories regarding the labyrinth?

Some factual inaccuracies get repeated over and over, until they take on the aura of facts. Keith Critchlow, a scholar in London with whom I have studied sacred geometry, wrote some things in 1972 which are now widely repeated as fact but are actually mistaken. He said that the labyrinth design is based on the geometry of an invisible thirteen-pointed star. Not so. He admits it doesn't "measure out," but he likes the symbolism (thirteen equals Jesus plus twelve disciples, counting Judas, and forgetting that the cathedral is dedicated to Mary). Critchlow also proposed that the rose window, if hinged down, would line up precisely with the labyrinth. Also not the case. The date of construction is another matter of contention. I believe that the labyrinth was built in 1201 because I accept the extensive research of John James on the subject. In her book, Lauren Artress uses the year 1220. I saw a website that said 1230, but then, it also said the labyrinth was made of blue and white stones. Wrong. Craig Wright is way off in his theory that the labyrinth was an afterthought. One French scholar wrote that the labyrinth is elliptical. Even something as basic as the size of the labyrinth seems to be a matter of conjecture. I guess it just isn't willing to be captured in literal terms. Its use is also a matter of speculation. For example, there is no record that it was ever used as a substitute for pilgrimage to the Holy Land.

Are there different ways to walk the labyrinth?

Yes, different ways and different reasons. How one walks the labyrinth depends somewhat on the intent and the occasion. Besides being used for meditation and prayer, labyrinths are ideal opportunities to overtly and clearly express our intent. We have organized walks, for example, for becoming clear on our direction in life during a period of transition. In such a case, one walks the labyrinth with a request in mind, like a mantra, repeating a phrase such as, "Show me the way, I will follow." Thus, walking the labyrinth becomes an exercise in surrendering, in allowing Spirit to lead us. Jill Geoffrion, a very mystical person, has authored a book with many suggestions for ways to walk the labyrinth (*Living the Labyrinth: 101 Paths to a Deeper Connection with the Sacred*). Some people walk for problem solving, or for enhancing creativity. I have seen people walking two steps forward then one step back, a pattern used in the Middle Ages. And of course, if you are under twelve years old, you generally run the labyrinth.

Doesn't Dr. Artress describe a way to walk the labyrinth?

Yes, she outlines a three-step method, the elements of which date back to the early Middle Ages: Purgation, illumination, and union. Purgation is experienced on the way to the center, during which we shed our concerns, our stumbling blocks, our tension and distraction. From it we can derive the word, to *purge*. Once we reach the center, we meditate, wherein we communicate with the divine, receiving illumination, clarity, insight. The final step is union. I think of it as *comm*union. It is the application and integration of the insights we received in the center, when we go back to our everyday lives. Sometimes these steps are given the modern words release, receive, and return.

In Chartres, is the labyrinth part of a larger procession?

Yes, and so it should be. While anything that is healing and beneficial is certainly appropriate all by itself, the labyrinth can be used effectively as a spiritual tool by incorporating ritual. Veriditas sponsors events each year in Chartres, in which they process through the candlelit crypt and around the cathedral before approaching the labyrinth. In other places, people sometimes walk around the perimeter of the labyrinth prior to walking it. Of course things are different in Chartres because it is such an amazing place. The whole cathedral is part of the experience. Sister Ann-Marie, before her retirement, led labyrinth walks in Chartres in which everyone walked single file in close procession. After reaching the center, they walked out the top of the labyrinth and continued to the altar, the final destination.

How receptive is Chartres to labyrinth walks?

Slowly things have been opening up. In 1997, on a pilgrimage to Chartres that I organized for Veriditas, we decided to raise the money to invite Francois Legaux, then rector of Chartres Cathedral, to San Francisco to see Grace Cathedral. There he saw two labyrinths that were open to the public, used in ways he found respectful and relevant. Since then, the labyrinth in Chartres has been uncovered most Fridays, and available upon request (and payment) by acceptable groups. Still, access is always tenuous as policies could change.

Is there a connection between the labyrinth and sacred geometry?

Sacred geometry was incorporated into the designs for the labyrinth and the cathedral. It was because of my labyrinth work that I initially pursued the study of sacred geometry. It is a fascinating subject which is not well known. Nothing was chosen at random. All the measurements used in the labyrinth had specific meaning and symbolism.

What are the underlying principles of sacred geometry?

When I first heard the term, I thought it must be about mathematics. Actually, it is more about philosophy and theology. Sacred geometry involves studying the physical universe in order to discover the principles that God used in Creation. Since nature is lawful, those laws must have been set into being by the Creator. The most basic elements of creation, right down to the nature of atoms themselves, rely on geometric shapes, which form a kind of universal language of numbers and proportions. This language spans centuries, even millennia, culture, language, and religion.

So sacred geometry incorporates certain numbers and proportions?

Yes, since long before we had modern mathematics. In sacred geometry, every number or proportion has a referent in the physical world. Once mathematics got into negative and theoretical numbers, there was no longer a connection to reality – one might say it lost its soul. In ancient times, only a few selected people understood how to use numbers. Even multiplication and division, known by every grade school child today, were very esoteric and complicated tasks until just a few centuries ago. Whenever I teach the basics of sacred geometry, people always come up to me afterwards and say, "Why don't they teach *that* in schools today?" In effect, numbers have a quality to them, not just quantity.

What are the basic principles of sacred geometry?

First, there is the assumption that the universe was created, and not a result of chance. Secondly, the lawfulness of the creation came from the Divine Mind. Third, if we study nature, we can discover those principles, numbers and proportions. Finally, we can then use those same principles in our own creations, such as cathedrals and labyrinths. Many books on sacred geometry fail to explain what is so sacred about it. The answer is simple: God originated it.

Can you give an example of qualities for numbers?

The number 3 is identified with the Trinity, the soul, and spirit, whereas 4 is identified with the body, the physical, the world, such as the four cardinal directions. Combining 3 and 4 means integrating body and soul, joining the holy and the mundane, which is the purpose of religion and spirituality. These numbers can be combined by adding (3 + 4 = 7) or multiplying (3 x 4 = 12), resulting in 7 and 12, both of which are extremely mystical numbers in all traditions. The numbers 3, 4, 7, and 12 are expressed in the geometry of the labyrinth. In architecture, too. The nave of Chartres Cathedral has seven bays (arches), which are divided by the labyrinth into groups of 3 and 4.

How else are numbers symbolized in the labyrinth?

Well, take the center of the labyrinth for example. There are six petals, so people assign them meanings such as the six days of Creation. Actually, it is based on a specific geometric shape. When you draw a circle, without changing the compass you can draw six identical circles around the first one, all of them just touching each other. The total figure incorporates seven circles. Seven is a very unique number. In the numbers 1 through 10, it is the only one that neither generates nor is generated by any other number. Hence it has been called "the virgin." Knowing this, the builders of the Chartres labyrinth designed the center based on a geometry of seven, since the cathedral is dedicated to the Virgin Mary. However, they stylized the petals rather than making them full circles, so the center circle is not apparent. A bronze plaque once occupied the middle circle.

What was on the central plaque?

The central plaque portrayed the story of Theseus slaying the Minotaur–the Greek legend. Today, people find that surprising. But in the Middle Ages, all of history, real or mythological, was seen as the precursor to the Christian era. That myth has caught the imagination of artists and scholars right up to modern times. Most interpreters say that Theseus represents Christ, slaying sin. I don't agree, as Christ wouldn't have needed assistance from Ariadne. I think Theseus represents each of us, the spiritual seeker, overcoming the dangers of the world and his or her darker impulses. As such, the story is archetypal, representing an underlying condition of what it means to be human. Ariadne's thread would be the teachings of the church, which give us guidance. The plaque was removed during the Napoleonic Wars and melted down to make cannon balls. I guess that's the opposite of the biblical instruction to beat our swords into plowshares.

What do the little circles around the perimeter of the labyrinth mean?

Dr. Lauren Artress has popularized Critchlow's term "lunations." The French simply call them "teeth" or "cogs" because it rather looks like a large gear wheel. "Lunations" makes sense because there are 112 of the partial circles, which comprise four symbolic 28-day lunar months. Remember that Easter is the first Sunday after the first full moon after the spring equinox. But I don't think it is a literal calculator. Throughout the cathedral we find images of sun and moon, representing Jesus and Mary. The length of the entire cathedral, in the unit of measure used at the time, is 365 and 1/4 feet – a solar calendar. This is balanced by the labyrinth with its lunar numbers, one more instance of the fact that the cathedral is dedicated to Mary (or, more precisely, to Mary's assumption into heaven). Hence, *Notre Dame* (our Lady). By the way, the two towers have a difference in height of 28 feet. The taller north tower has a weathervane with a sun on it, the other tower has a weathervane with a moon.

Does the feminine aspect of the labyrinth represent Mary?

I think it is broader than that. Mary represents more than just being the mother of Jesus. She is a feminine archetype. So is the labyrinth. The labyrinth by nature is very feminine. The labyrinth is round, it takes us into itself, it is embracing, nourishing. I think that's one of its attractions in our out-of-balance masculine culture. Further, in the path of the labyrinth, there are 277 stones, which represent the number of days of human gestation (nine months) and the time from the Annunciation (March 25th) to Christmas. From the symbolism for birth it is only a short step to the symbolism of rebirth and transformation. In that regard, I feel the feminine nature of the labyrinth plays an important role. As the Catholic priesthood was (and is) exclusively male, perhaps the labyrinth was an attempt to introduce something more feminine, to make Mary's home on earth more welcoming and suitable.

How did you find these meanings hidden in the labyrinth?

Some of it is based on my own original discoveries and research. With regards to the geometry of Chartres Cathedral, and many aspects of Gothic in particular, I owe much to the astounding work of John James. In the 1970's he spent six years studying Chartres Cathedral stone by stone. His work, which has now carried over to other Gothic buildings, has rewritten some of what we understand on the subject. He believes that the labyrinth was built in 1201 by the same mason who laid out the cathedral, who certainly would have been the greatest master of his era. That means the labyrinth wasn't merely a decoration or an afterthought, but an important part of the overall plan. The same mason made the magnificent western rose window, fifteen years later.

Nothing was left to chance in the building of Chartres?

The masons didn't just pick their measurements by whim or random. Everything is related to everything else. As already mentioned, in the nave of the cathedral, the labyrinth divides the nave into three bays and four bays. The ratio of the width to the height of the nave is 4:7. There are many other numbers and proportions, of course, in addition to these, especially transcendent and irrational numbers such as *pi* or the square roots of 2, 3, and 5. These numbers can't be calculated definitively by mathematics, even using computers. But they can be easily drawn, geometrically, and represented, physically.

So there's a lot more going on than meets the eye.

Yes, and a lot that *does* meet the eye. When you enter Chartres, regardless of how huge it is, it doesn't crush you. It feels friendly, welcoming. In later cathedrals, like Amiens, the immensity seems overwhelming, without a personal touch. That's why Chartres is so unique. It's true with the labyrinth, as well – just looking at it can be rewarding. In fact, "walking" a labyrinth with your eyes can be just as powerful as doing it with your body. Watching other people walk the labyrinth can also be very calming. While I think it is helpful to know the mechanics and principles behind the cathedral and the labyrinth, such knowledge isn't a prerequisite for using and enjoying them.

But more knowledge can deepen the experience.

Certainly. It's like studying the Bible. If you have visited the cities that are mentioned in the scripture, or if you know details about the lives of the people in the stories, the meaning is greatly enhanced. You become personally involved rather than just being an observer. The more I learn about Chartres Cathedral and the labyrinth, the more I realize how much remains to be discovered. When you walk the labyrinth, you aren't reading about it or theorizing about it, you're actually *doing* something. And by doing something, you receive something real in return. The intellectual component can enhance the experience, or it can be a hindrance. As a labyrinth maker, for example, I sometimes get sidetracked by noticing the elements of construction rather than concentrating on my walking. Ever since Chartres Cathedral was built, there have been tour guides, to help people understand what they are seeing and its relevance. I was such a guide, for seventeen years. I think my groups left with a greater appreciation of what they were experiencing.

You're saying to walk your talk.

I saw one labyrinth event advertised as "Taking a stroll with your soul." I've used that title a couple of times. Not only do we walk our talk, which is to say, practice what we preach, but we also walk our walk. We all have a certain amount of walking to do, to get where we are going. The key to spiritual practice is exactly that: practice. Repetition. The labyrinth gives us a means through which to find the sacred. It's not just a metaphor for life, it *is* life. Historically, the labyrinth has been used for rituals that mark passages through life, from birth to death, and even after death. Labyrinths on ancient tombs may have been symbolic maps to help the deceased negotiate the twists and turns of the afterlife. Technically, the labyrinth itself is made of lines, whereas we walk the paths, between the lines. With books, reading between the lines refers to finding the true, some-times hidden meaning. The same is true for labyrinths, which serve as devices for guiding us on our inner journeys.

How do you use a labyrinth to mark life's passages?

Labyrinths lend themselves to ceremony and ritual. Our society does very little in recognizing important passages in life. In *Labyrinths from the Outside In,* Donna Schaper and Carole Ann Camp have several chapters suggesting labyrinth rituals and ceremonies, including: Walks for Rites of Passage, Walks for the Four Seasons, Walking in Many Spiritual Traditions, and Walks for the Celtic Year and the Zodiac. Similarly, in *The Way of the Labyrinth,* Helen Curry describes ceremonies for weddings and rituals throughout the year. Recently, at a bon voyage party for a couple leaving to tour Europe, each guest was given a "passport" which was stamped at different points throughout the labyrinth. In the center was a model of the

Eiffel Tower. I don't see why labyrinths couldn't be used to similarly celebrate saint's days, church holidays, confirmation, baptism, marriage, and other steps along the spiritual journey.

Are labyrinths used with children?

Absolutely! There is a very active movement based on using labyrinths in schools, with a number of books on the subject. The Labyrinth Resource Group in Santa Fe has been a leader in this area (see www.labyrinthresourcegroup.org). One facilitator I know takes a small labyrinth to a grade school once a month. The teacher says there has been a noticeable improvement in the kids; they are more focused, less rambunctious. They look forward to each labyrinth visit. Another teacher has her kids trace finger labyrinths prior to taking tests. She says it calms and focuses them. Many schools have outdoor labyrinths. Of course kids usually run and play on the labyrinths. I know of a teacher who has a class of students with serious behavior difficulties. She has a small canvas labyrinth in the back of the classroom. During class, if a student gets antsy sitting still, he or she is given permission to walk the labyrinth while still listening to the teacher. Disruptions have greatly decreased.

What do you think attracts kids to labyrinths?

For one thing, it's a boost to their self esteem because everyone wins. It's not a competition. With kids, the labyrinth can teach motor skills and coordination. When young people reach the center, they beam proudly for having accomplished their goal. As long as they stay on the path, they can't fail. In fact, success is a factor for all walkers. One author calls the labyrinth "user friendly." Kids learn about cooperation while walking with others. Our first studio for making canvas labyrinths was in an art school that catered to inner city kids, most of whom were very unruly. One day, they came outside where we had a labyrinth on the grass. They didn't walk it properly, in adult terms. They ran around and elbowed each other and strayed from path to path. Then they went back into class. The teacher asked us the next day, "What did you do to those kids?" She said they were calmer, more attentive and easier to teach. At a church school in California, parents have learned to bring their children ten minutes earlier, so they can spend time on the labyrinth before going into class. The kids enjoy it, and the teachers reap the benefits.

Do children ever walk the labyrinth meditatively?

Sure. We have seen that many times. Often, after running around for a while, they slow down and get more focused. A little girl once asked me, "Do we pray before we walk or when we reach the center?" Once, during a labyrinth dedication at a public park in Illinois, I mentioned the fact that kids eventually slow down. I noticed the audience was amused. Turning around, I saw three children who had been playing on the labyrinth, now walking it calmly and with concentration.

What have been some of your favorite labyrinth walks?

Of course, walking in Chartres Cathedral is incomparable. At dusk the windows slowly lose their brilliance. Walking at night in candlelight is also very moving. On New Year's Eve, 1999, we made a labyrinth out of luminaries, paper bags with gravel and votive candles in them. They glowed like Japanese lanterns and lasted for hours, into the early hours of the morning of the new year. Some of my best experiences have been on very simple backyard labyrinths. Church labyrinths have the added attraction of a beautiful setting.

Do you keep a record of your walks?

We recommend several ways to record one's labyrinth experience. If you provide a notebook for people to write comments, you will accumulate a body of quotations that can be quite impressive and moving. Most authors of labyrinth books generously sprinkle their works with the wisdom of people who have expressed themselves in such guest books. One labyrinth facilitator at a hospital in Oregon has the organizer of each event fill out a simple form describing their purpose and process. She showed me a stack of forms describing an amazing variety of uses. Websites and social media offer another outlet for sharing labyrinth activities.

Are there dangers in walking labyrinths?

I haven't heard a single report of anyone who walked a labyrinth and found that it ruined their life. Sometimes, nothing seems to happen. If people come to the labyrinth with high expectations that aren't met to their satisfaction, a feeling of disappointment may result. I've heard people say there is no right or wrong way to walk a labyrinth. That's silly. I can think of many wrong ways. How about playing cymbals and shoving other people out of your way, for example. It's better to say that nothing is *supposed* to happen.

Is there no assurance that anything will happen in a labyrinth?

One man called me and asked if he bought a portable canvas labyrinth from me would I guarantee that it would "work." Questioning him further, I found that he had certain expectations that he felt must be fulfilled or else he would want a refund. I suggested that if the labyrinth didn't "work," that might be a very valuable lesson, which would mean that it did work. He didn't understand my point, nor did he buy anything. I think something always happens, but we may not notice what it is. Experience from walking a labyrinth is cumulative. Perhaps after ten walks, something important will happen. Were the prior nine walks failures? Of course not. If the walker gave up after five walks, the future benefit would be lost.

Do people ever get upset walking the labyrinth?

Tears are quite common, but usually they don't come from being upset. Older people sometimes find balance to be a problem, or the pattern to be confusing. Once in a post-walk sharing, a participant said that she didn't like the labyrinth, but she wasn't upset. My general recommendation is to follow an unpleasant experience on the labyrinth with another walk. Usually the next walk is completely different, often giving clarity to the issue at hand. The labyrinth serves as a magnifier for us to see things about our lives that we have been missing.

If the labyrinth magnifies our "issues," can't that be problematic?

My personal belief is that the labyrinth is a very gentle and personal tool. Perhaps someone could become aware of an issue that she would rather not face, but I find the labyrinth to be self-regulating. You will have whatever experience you are ready to handle. It never forces itself on anyone. Generally speaking, seeing our issues is a good thing, although not everyone may feel that way. Professional labyrinth facilitators are trained to help counsel people who have had poignant experiences on the labyrinth. I believe all labyrinth walks should have a time of sharing afterwords, to deal with any difficulty someone might have. This can be done in a group, or by having docents available individually.

Are there people who oppose the labyrinth?

I know of individual cases in which people oppose the labyrinth and are upset that other people are walking it. In one dramatic case, opponents within the church burned the portable canvas labyrinth, destroying it. Usually, opposition is based on mistaken advice, with the opponents having never walked it themselves. After one fundamentalist opponent was assured that the labyrinth came from Chartres Cathedral, he continued to disapprove, saying, "That's *Catholic*" (whereas he was Protestant). A few websites oppose the labyrinth, usually decrying that it is not biblical. How biblical are cars, or shopping malls? Others say labyrinths are pagan. I ask if they have music in their churches. Pagans, you know, use music to dance naked by the light of the moon. To me, those who oppose the labyrinth are the very people who should walk them. One woman to whom I spoke on an airplane was opposed to meditation of any kind because she had been told if you empty your mind, the devil will occupy it.

How does one respond to such opposition?

I don't think it's possible. Such folks aren't going to be convinced by argument. Confrontation is often their whole *modus operandi,* seeing themselves as defending their narrow beliefs. If people don't like the labyrinth, they can choose not to walk it. Going further and saying that no one should walk it is going too far, in my opinion. I am reminded of the poem "Outwitted" by Edwin Markham:

> He drew a circle that shut me out.
> Heretic, rebel, a thing to flout.
> But love and I had wit to win.
> We drew a circle that took him in.

The labyrinth is an inclusive circle, whether its opponents want to be included or not.

Buying a labyrinth can be an important financial decision for a church.

While some labyrinths can seem rather expensive, other types can be built for almost nothing. Rarely is such a purchase a sudden event, however. Usually some of the church people walk a labyrinth elsewhere, form a committee, and start preparing the ground to have their own labyrinth. Perhaps they will have someone bring a portable labyrinth to their church so that people can see it and watch how it is used. Someone can give a presentation, showing slides of labyrinths and describing their history. Some churches own a portable canvas labyrinth first, and later decide to build a permanent outdoor labyrinth. Many labyrinths are donated as memorials for loved ones. Compared to what some amenities cost, a labyrinth is actually very cost effective.

Explain again how the labyrinth works.

It works by leading us to ourselves. There's a saying that says, "In a maze you lose yourself, but in a labyrinth, you find yourself." What a discovery! It's hard to find God out in the world of smoke and mirrors. Better to go inside, to be quiet, attentive. It's good to ask for guidance, for Spirit to help us. Then, we have to be silent enough and open enough to hear the answer. Praying is asking, meditating is listening–both happen in the labyrinth. The labyrinth works by rescuing us from of our busy lives. When walking a labyrinth, we aren't checking things off on our "to do" list. Nor, hopefully, are we conducting business (although I once saw a man walking a labyrinth while talking on his cell phone). Even getting to the center is no big challenge. Walking is not about reaching the destination, it's about the quality of the journey. The point is, we are spending time with ourselves. Quality time. Sacred time. When we spend time with our authentic selves, we get closer to God, in whose image we are made. As a result, we may rearrange the priorities in our lives to be more rewarding and meaningful. Even dancing or playing on the labyrinth can be a sacred experience, healthy for our souls. The labyrinth is the threshold to our inner world. Much is to be discovered there.

How can a church know if the labyrinth is right for them?

That's hard to tell. My suggestion would be to start slowly and not make a big commitment until a certain amount of value has been perceived. It is possible to rent labyrinths, or borrow portable ones from other churches. Several denominational offices have bought portable labyrinths from me, which they share among the different churches in their region. In fact, in one instance the labyrinth was booked so far in advance that they bought a second, then a third, and ultimately a fourth labyrinth. It is also possible to make inexpensive temporary labyrinths, by mowing them in the lawn, painting the grass, putting masking tape on the floor, and so on. Temporary labyrinths can be used to raise funds for buying a permanent one.

How much do labyrinths cost?

That's like asking how much a car costs. That depends. I have built labyrinths with budgets ranging from a thousand dollars to a quarter of a million dollars. Labyrinths are complex and time-consuming to make, therefore labor intensive. Making your own with volunteers resolves the labor expense, but often with mixed results, depending on your volunteers and their level of expertise. Purchasing a portable labyrinth costs from one to four thousand dollars. Do-it-yourself labyrinths are generally made from materials such as stones and mulch. These can be made for one to three thousand dollars. They are likely to be high maintenance and not accessible to wheel-chairs.   Mowing a labyrinth into the grass costs next to nothing. Permanent hard surface concrete labyrinths, installed by profession-als such as ourselves, start somewhere in the thirty thousand dollar range. Paver and stone labyrinths cost twice that, and up into six figures. To this you add the cost of amenities, such as benches, water features, lighting, and landscaping.

Do you have any suggestions for fundraising?

I have one important suggestion: Make the commitment first, and the money will follow. When I hear people say, "Oh, we're putting our money away little by little, hoping someday to be able to have enough for a labyrinth," I worry about their success. Yes, sometimes it takes a while. But what I think is most effective is to decide on the labyrinth you want, right down to the location, the design, the ma-terials, installation cost and amenities. Make a brochure with a drawing or photos of similar labyrinths, saying, "This is our laby-rinth." Seeing this, donors can get inspired. More than forty percent of our labyrinths have been paid for by one or two donors who wrote large checks as memorials to loved ones. Some labyrinths were part of a larger project, such as a prayer garden, columbarium, or courtyard renovation. When building a new church, or an addi-tion, put the labyrinth right into the budget. In all cases, assume success.

How long does it take to raise enough money?

I have known some labyrinth fundraising campaigns to take several years. The record, in my experience, is held by a doctor in Australia who worked for eleven years to get a labyrinth at his hospital. He kept at it until he succeeded. On the other hand, the shortest time we have experienced was about two months, from initial concept to completion. One church put an appeal in the Sunday bulletin and raised the money the following week. Another church had just finished a large capital campaign. They were skeptical that people would give yet again for a labyrinth. The minister told the church, "The money we just spent was for the infrastructure, the buildings and the physical assets. The labyrinth is for you directly, for your spiritual life. You can call it 'Inner-structure'." Further, they went to the community and said, "This public labyrinth will benefit you, too." Between the church and the town, they raised the money easily.

Is a labyrinth cost efficient?

Even if you buy a work of art built to last for generations costing well into six figures, I believe the value is there. Relative to what everything else costs these days for construction, the labyrinth is often the least expensive element in a project. We have seen landscaping cost many times what the labyrinth did. Once the labyrinth is built, many churches are pleased to see how frequently it is used. One church reports that it is rare for a day to go by without looking out and seeing someone walking the labyrinth. It makes a great addition to any church ministry. Unlike a building or some activity, the labyrinth needs no staff other than a minimum of care and maintenance. As a one time expense amortized over any years, it is quite cost effective.

Do some churches build their own labyrinth?

In some cases, especially regarding temporary labyrinths. In a few cases I've seen, they gave the responsibility to someone who was unfamiliar with labyrinths, with unfortunate results. So I recommend that in a do-it-yourself situation, someone must be familiar with the task at hand. You could hire a professional labyrinth maker to supervise, if necessary. Kits are available for paver labyrinths, which again have mixed results. For permanent, hard surface, wheelchair accessible labyrinths, the materials and techniques are often too advanced for volunteers. Currently our most popular labyrinth is made of crushed granite overlay on a concrete base. The base is poured by a local contractor. The installation of the labyrinth pattern, however, is done in a way that is friendly to volunteers. So, we send one experienced labyrinth artist to guide the process, while most of the work is done by the church members and volunteers. Besides saving money, using volunteers also builds community.

How durable are such labyrinths?

We promise two things about concrete: It won't burn and it will crack. Eventually. Sometimes cracks become visible very soon, whereas for some concrete it takes years. Such blemishes in no way detract from the effective use of the labyrinth. However, poor concrete can have a deleterious affect on the labyrinth pattern that rests on it. Any spalling or efflorescence or breaking up of the concrete will hurt the labyrinth. That being said, the vast majority of the labyrinths we have made in the past seventeen years are still functional and going strong. Paint or stain have a limited lifetime, usually not more than five to ten years. That's why we developed polymer concrete and crushed granite overlay, which should last indefinitely. Examples are available in the gallery section of our website at www.labyrinth-enterprises.com/ourwork.html.

How do we find a professional labyrinth installer?

The easiest way is to contact me personally at my email, which is robert@labyrinth-enterprises.com. While I am officially retired, and even though I am pushing 70, I stay involved in the labyrinth business. My goal is to turn Labyrinth Enterprises, LLC, into a collaborative which includes many labyrinth artists with all the skills needed to create the perfect labyrinth for every situation. Only rarely do I personally install a labyrinth, but I am available for consultation on a fee basis, usually by telephone or email. Another excellent source of information is the Labyrinth Society website at (www.labyrinthsociety.com). My recommendations can be seen in the resources section at the end of the book.

Will churches continue to use labyrinths?

Yes, I think so. There will always be a need for sacred space, for prayer and meditation, for rituals and ceremonies. Perhaps some day labyrinths will be considered a standard feature in churches – you have a sanctuary, a chapel, an organ, a labyrinth. Nor will they be alone. We continue to build labyrinths in other venues as well, such as hospitals (including a growing number of VA hospitals), public parks, universities, retirement centers, and private estates. When I first started in this work, labyrinths were unknown and hard to find. Now they are everywhere. Of course the semantic confusion between labyrinths and mazes continues, especially on the internet. I think labyrinths are here to stay, for which we are all the better.

Appendix I

The following section contains quotations from a number of books available in 2001 for the first edition of this book. The passages were chosen for their relevance to the topic of churches. All of these books contain a far broader range of material than what I have quoted. I encourage you to buy them and read them in their entirety. There are, of course, many more books available now about labyrinths, which also deserve to be quoted here. I will leave such research to the reader.

Walking a Sacred Path: Rediscovering the Labyrinth as a Spiritual Tool
The Rev. Dr. Lauren Artress
Riverhead Books, New York, 1995 – ISBN: 1-57322-007-8

[Note: This was one of the first contemporary books on labyrinths. The Rev. Dr. Lauren Artress is an Episcopal priest and founder of Veriditas, which is described in the Resources section.]

"During a retreat, I stumbled across an ancient mystical tool called the labyrinth, which had dropped out of human awareness more than 350 years ago. I first began to research the labyrinth and then later to introduce it to people at Grace Cathedral and in workshops around the country. I moved from curiosity to skepticism to profound respect for the uncanny gifts of insight, wisdom, and peace the labyrinth offers. It connects us to the depths of our souls so we can remember who we are."

"The labyrinth is a spiritual tool meant to awaken us to the deep rhythm that unites us to ourselves and to the Light that calls from within. In surrendering to the winding path, the soul finds healing and wholeness."

"Based on the circle, the universal symbol for unity and wholeness, the labyrinth sparks the human imagination and introduces it to a kaleidoscopic patterning that builds a sense of relationship: one person to another, to another, to many people, to creation of the whole. It enlivens the intuitive part of our nature and stirs within the human heart the longing for connectedness and the remembrance of our purpose for living."

"Why does the labyrinth attract people? Because it is a tool to guide healing, deepen self-knowledge, and empower creativity. Walking the labyrinth clears the mind and gives insight into the spiritual journey. It urges action. It calms people in the throes of life transitions. It helps them see their lives in the context of a path, a pilgrimage."

"The labyrinth introduces us to the idea of a wide and gracious path. It redefines the journey to God: from a vertical perspective that goes from earth up to heaven, to a horizontal perspective in which we are all walking the path together. The vertical path has gotten mired down in perfectionist associations, whereas the horizontal path communicates that we are all in this together."

"People have revelatory experiences in the labyrinth . . .. Seekers frequently meet their spiritual longing, are greeted by velvety silence, or hear the still, small voice within. They gain wisdom, assurance, solace, peace, and direction."

"The labyrinth can play a significant role in the field of spiritual direction. It can guide people to glimpses of the Divine. It can help people reach spiritual maturity."

"In essence, the winding path of the labyrinth offers a blueprint for the psyche to meet the soul."

"The labyrinth is unusual because it is an archetype with which we can have direct experience in the outer world. We can literally walk it. Usually archetypes are psychological processes that other people cannot see or experience along with us. . .. The archetype that is enlivened in the labyrinth is the archetype of transformation. . .. When we contact an archetype, it is like releasing a time capsule in the psyche. We contact the power of the numinous. Jung described it 'as though chords in us were struck that had never resounded before, or as though forces whose existence we never suspected were un- loosed.' The breadth of life is breathed back into us, and we are spurred on to live life more fully."

"The labyrinth was designed by an intelligence we cannot fully un- derstand. But this much I do know. The labyrinth is truly a tool for transformation. It is a crucible for change . . . a field of light, a cos- mic dance. It is a center for empowering ritual. It is a container where we can meet angels and recover the great-grandmother's thread, the web of Mary, and the gracious, nurturing God."

"The labyrinth is truly a tool for our times. It can help us find our way through the bewildering multiplicity, to the unity of source. The labyrinth is an evocative experience. The labyrinth provides the sacred space where the inner and outer worlds can commune, where thinking mind and imaginative heart can flow together. It can pro- vide a space to listen to our inner voice of wisdom and come to grip with our role in humankind's next evolutionary step. Troubled communities can come to the labyrinth to discover and synchronize their vision. It gives us a glimpse of other realms and other ways of knowing."

"Many people have reported seeing angels around the labyrinth. And although I rarely see into the invisible world, I often feel a soft and graceful air around the labyrinth."

◆ ◆ ◆ ◆ ◆

Labyrinths From the Outside In: Walking to Spiritual Insight, a Beginner's Guide
Donna Schaper and Carole Ann Camp
Skylight Paths Publishing, Woodstock, VT, 2000 – ISBN:1-893361-18-7

[Note: Written by two Protestant clergy, this book contains much ma- terial that pertains directly to church use of labyrinths.]

"In labyrinths, whether ancient or modern, we walk in and we walk out. We coil and we uncoil. We do so both physically and spiritually.

The body and the spirit experience an intentional, simultaneous outing. We walk a path. It is both a spiritual path and a physical path – not either/or, but both/and. Our spiritual journey and our physical journey are united. When walking the labyrinth, we get comfort because we find ourselves on the Way. We do not have to act as if it is the same way for all people. Instead, we should think of it as our way."

"The labyrinth lets people walk together and separately without agreeing on everything. The very ancient nature of the labyrinth combined with the archetypal metaphor of its design draws us to absolutes that transcend any human constructs that have separated humanity into arbitrary religious categories for centuries. That is why labyrinths are so welcome today; they allow each of us to find our own center in our own way."

" . . . people need spiritual aids, things, or pictures to help them find God. The labyrinth is an exquisite thing, which is used imaginatively as a thing or an object to help us find God."

"Walking the labyrinth is a metaphysical, not a physical, practice – but it cannot be *meta* until it is *physical*. One of the strongest appeals of the labyrinth is that it is a spirituality connected to a body. We do not have to leave our bodies behind to walk the labyrinth. They come with us."

"One of the big words in modern theology is *embodiment*. People want to know if we can walk the walk as well as talk the talk: labyrinths answer that question yes, if in ever so modest a way. Labyrinths encourage embodiment rather than discourage it; that is a strong reason for their popularity among new seekers."

"Labyrinths are, however, more spiritual than religious. They offer a distinction between religion and spirituality. They embody spirituality, not religion, and many people are 'allergic' to religion today."

"I asked my teenagers if there was a difference between spirituality and religion. . ... The sixteen-year-old said, 'In church you have to sit there – in spirituality, you can move around.' My fourteen-year-old came along for the ride: 'In religion, it's all God, God, God, and how God is good and we're bad. In spirituality, there is room for us.'"

"Labyrinth walking is one way to be pious, to have a spiritual practice without having to carry the burden of centuries of traditional religious authority – the centuries-old complex of liturgies and prayers, hymns and linens, the gestures and habits of all our various faiths – simple labyrinth walking opens up piety as a point of view of life, of a way to be in the world. . ... Labyrinths are one of many wonderful devices for practicing the presence of God, but they are hardly the only one."

"The gift of the labyrinth in my life is that it has restored my spiritual sense of humor. It has given me a kind of clarity about how 'large' God is. It has also given me a sense of how much life truly is a journey, a movement, or a process: from every point in the labyrinth, God and life look different."

"Cultivating the inner is the best way to find the beauty of the human soul. Labyrinths cultivate the inner, which is the site of our authority. For our spiritual rest and recreation, we may walk a labyrinth, run one, or dance one."

"Walking around in patterned circles can be good for the soul. It can be good for the fruits, or consequences, of one's life: inner health gives outer capacity. However, some people get stuck inside and they prefer to stay there. Some people internalize, believing that the inner or internal life is the only life. One of the most important messages of the labyrinth is the combination of the inward and outward journeys; they are the same path."

"The labyrinth helps me to do something with everybody that I do not have to do *right*. In helps me to hear the ancient texts in a new way."

"[In walking a labyrinth] a choice has been made, a spiritual discipline has been chosen; the presence of Spirit is being sought. Making the choice and taking the first step into the labyrinth is to risk discovering the mystery at the very center of our being. The good thing about labyrinths is that you cannot make a mistake. There are no wrong turns. You cannot get lost. Symbolically what could be better than knowing that by staying on the path, by following all the turns, you will eventually find the center – the Holy of Holies?"

◆ ◆ ◆ ◆ ◆

The Way of the Labyrinth: A Powerful Meditation for Everyday Life

Helen Curry
Penguin Compass, New York, 2000 – ISBN: 0-14-019617-X

[Note: Helen Curry was the first president of the Labyrinth Society.]

From the Foreword by Jean Houston:

"As a young girl in New York City, I used to walk in Central Park with an old man I had met by chance. I called him Mr. Tayer, and he turned out to be Teillard de Chardin, the great philosopher, poet, paleontologist, and mystic. The last time I saw him, in April 1955, I brought him the shell of a snail. 'Ah, escargot,' he exclaimed and then proceeded to wax ecstatic for the better part of an hour on the presence of spirals in nature and art. Snail shells and galaxies, the meanderings of rivers, the circulation of the heart's blood, and the labyrinth on the floor of Chartres Cathedral were taken up into a great hymn to the spiraling evolution of spirit and matter. That was how I first learned about the labyrinth in Chartres Cathedral, although it wasn't until years later that I visited there and experienced the power of that great journey in stone."

"For me the great work of the labyrinth is the challenge to leave the center-point and return outward to perform deep, loving service to the world, carrying the gifts and knowings of this visit to the heart of things."

"Something about the turnings of the labyrinth releases us from the tyranny of the local and the habitual. I believe that release is something we all seek. We are at a point in time in which everything is in transition, the maps no longer fit any of the territories, and the territories no longer fit any of the maps. But there are certain sureties, certain patterns in mind and body, spirit and nature, and the labyrinth is one. It allows us a map that is not a map, a journey that transcends journey, and gives a kind of clarity to our lives that we cannot find through ordinary means."

Quotations from Helen Curry:

"People all over the world are discovering that the ancient practice of walking labyrinths not only solves problems, but also soothes the nerves, calms the soul, mends the heart, and heals the body. It can help bring us into balance, giving us a sense of wholeness that is much needed for all of us whose lives ache with lopsided discomfort . . .. Quite simply, labyrinths are a way to discover the sacred in everyday life."

"Labyrinths offer the opportunity to walk in meditation to that place within us where the rational merges with the intuitive and the spiritual is reborn."

"The beauty of the labyrinth walk is that it is open to anyone at any stage, on any spiritual path, and from any religious tradition. It is a symbol open to your intentions."

"Within the energy of the twists and turns, of the going into the center and coming back out again, people find resources within themselves that they never before knew they had."

"Weddings on the labyrinth are wonderful and have a completely different feeling than traditional weddings. Rather than the traditional walk down the 'straight and narrow' of the church aisle, the couple walk around the paths and turns of the labyrinth – a much more accurate metaphor for the journey they are embarking upon. Where many modern weddings seem to be rushed, the labyrinth slows down time. It also seems to connect the participants and observers to the sacred in a way that many modern weddings don't."

"The labyrinth is one of the most compassionate and humane meditation tools available. It accesses all parts of what it means to be human. It is sacred space, yet it uses the body to pass through its pathways. It is a meditational tool that makes profound heart connections, yet it engages the rational mind as well."

"I think the most important reason the labyrinth works is because of our intention. On some level, most labyrinth walkers, either consciously or unconsciously, go into a labyrinth walk ready to receive something even if they are very skeptical."

"It's not unusual for feelings of woundedness to come up during a labyrinth walk. The first reaction may be to recoil from the feelings. However, many experts suggest that such experiences are healing. Reopening these feelings, and looking at them anew, is better than pretending they don't exist. The labyrinth offers a safe haven to examine old wounds, to feel the pain that has been inflicted, and more often than not, to take the first steps toward healing . . .. The labyrinth walk can often bring up not only the wound, but also the means to heal that wound, to find a way to love the self and others . . .."

◆ ◆ ◆ ◆ ◆

Exploring the Labyrinth: A Guide for Healing and Spiritual Growth
Melissa Gayle West
Broadway Books, New York, 2000 – ISBN: 0-7679-0356-0

[Note: I was privileged to write the introduction to Melissa West's book.]

"Whoever you are, walking the labyrinth has something to offer you. If a creative or work project is challenging you, walking can get your creative juices flowing. When you are struggling with grief and anger or a physical challenge or illness, walking the labyrinth can point the way to healing and wholeness. If you're wanting a way to meditate or pray that engages your body as well as your soul, the labyrinth can be such a way. When you just want reflective time away from a busy life, the labyrinth can offer you time out. The labyrinth, as you will learn, holds up a mirror, reflecting back to us not only the light of our finest selves, but also whatever restrains us from shining forth."

"The labyrinth's gift is simplicity, both the simplicity of stripping away all external dos and don'ts to listen to our own voices, and the simplicity of the walk itself. No advanced degrees are necessary to walk the labyrinth, no long training sessions, no technical manuals. There are no 'levels' to complete, nothing to memorize, no tests to take. All that is really required in walking the labyrinth is to show up, place one foot in front of the other, and breathe."

"I have been deeply moved by how the labyrinth has taught cancer patients about wholeness, church congregations and board members of nonprofits about community, mourners about the healing of the heart, long-estranged family members about reconciliation. When walking the labyrinth we all – no matter how different our lives may be – become pilgrims together on the path to wholeness."

"Throughout human history we have sat in circles, danced in circles, drawn circles on everything from cave walls to contemporary canvases. Remember the pictures of suns – circles of light and Self – you made as a child. Know that whenever you step foot into the labyrinth, you are within that sacred circle."

"Walking the labyrinth doesn't just deepen intimacy with family and friends, however. It can be a powerful catalyst for opening to others we know little or not at all. I use labyrinths in as many workshops as I can. Walking the labyrinth can build community quickly, even in a group of strangers, cutting through the resistances to intimacy...."

◆ ◆ ◆ ◆ ◆

Praying the Labyrinth
Jill Kimberly Hartwell Geoffrion
The Pilgrim Press, Cleveland,1999 – ISBN: 0-8298-1343-8

[Note: Jill Geoffrion is the most mystical person I have ever met, who communes with the labyrinth and Chartres Cathedral on many, deep levels. Her writing is concise and poetic. She has numerous other books about the labyrinth. Her ministry takes the labyrinth to churches and seminaries in Third World countries such as Myanmar and the Democratic Republic of Congo.

Her website has spectacular photographs of her work, and Chartres Cathedral. See: www.jillgeoffrion.com.]

"I hear one of the facilitators of our pilgrimage saying,
'The labyrinth is your tool.'
I have known the labyrinth as
a way of prayer . . . a beautiful pattern of Truth . . . something ancient with modern relevance . . . one of God's dwelling places . . . a container for religious ritual . . .
but have never recognized it as one of my spiritual tools.
With this insight stoking the fires of my creativity,
I am filled with longing, hope, and most of all, excitement."

"The lecturer is speaking of the labyrinth as 'an incredibly powerful problem solving device.'
I have experienced what he means.
Yet the dynamism I feel in the labyrinth's presence
leads me to other expressions of this truth.
If I wanted to say something about using the labyrinth
to help solve a problem
I would suggest:
'The labyrinth is a place to be with a problem
in the energetic presence of the Divine.'"

"Tears gently stroke my cheeks as I consider Bernard of Clairvaux's poem. He wrote about his relationship with Jesus' mother;
his words speak to me of something very different.
'When you follow her, you cannot make a wrong turning;
When you pray to her, you cannot lose hope;
When she fills your thoughts, you are sheltered from all error;
When she holds you up, you cannot fall;
When she protects you, you are never afraid;
When she leads you forward, you are never tired;
When her grace shines on you, you arrive at your goal.'
I cry because at last I have heard the words
which express my experience of walking the labyrinth
and apprehending the beauty of God."

"Labyrinths are . . . symbols, spiritual tools, mathematical images, harmonic patterns, pathways of discovery, playgrounds of prayer."

On Jill Geoffrion's blog (throughjillseyes.wordpress.com) she shares this story:

"After class one day, I went up to the chapel to walk and pray. A student choir was rehearsing in the front by the piano. Their voices and Kachin song accompanied me as I moved on the labyrinth. When I was done, I continued my prayer as I looked out the fourth floor windows. Suddenly I was aware of someone beside me, "How do you do this?" the first year student asked. When I turned around I saw two other students already praying. I told her, "Let's walk together, I'll show you." She wasn't sure what to do when she got to the first turn, but with a little encouragement and a few basic instructions she was following the path on her own. In the center, I heard quiet sobbing. I prayed for her journey–on and off the labyrinth.

"Afterwards, she found me at the window again. "This prayer really changes us," she told me. "What did you experience?" I asked. "When I came I was only aware of my problems, but now I feel different." We talked about her concerns and her prayer. She told me she wanted to build a labyrinth at her church. I explained that next year I will be offering an elective class on labyrinth prayer which will include labyrinth construction, and invited her to take it. I hope she does!

"I love how God uses the labyrinth to touch people and to minister to their needs. Over and over again, I see God using labyrinth prayer to bring people together, to help us care for one another, and to inspire us to serve our communities in new ways."

♦ ♦ ♦ ♦ ♦

The Idea of the Labyrinth from Classical Antiquity through the Middle Ages
Penelope Reed Doob
Cornell University Press, Ithaca, 1990 – ISBN: 0-8014-8000-0

[Note: This scholarly book only peripherally mentions labyrinth use. One of the few scholarly books on the subject, it is often quoted.]

"Because the diagrammatic unicursal labyrinth exposes its structure and solves itself, it betokens controlled artistry; but because it achieves its end through disorientation and confusion, it differs from cathedral and *summa*: it represents also the difficulty of attaining clarity for artist and observer alike, whose eventual success is thereby rendered more impressive."

"Typical medieval mazes thus consist of a perfect form, the circle – the shape of the world, the universe, eternity. They are stamped with the cross, perhaps suggesting the impact of Christ on the world . . . . They combine two important principles: the path defines linear progress (the march of time, Christian history, of human life); the whole pattern illustrates circular perfection (the cosmos, eternity, liturgical and seasonal repetition and renewal). In this context . . . labyrinths in churches or other sacred contexts may fitly represent not only human but divine artistry or even the intersection of human and divine perspectives and actions."

"If secular labyrinths in aristocratic and popular culture alike tend to glorify the artistry of man, ecclesiastical labyrinths generally celebrate the triumphs of divine artistry and of human ingenuity in the service of God."

"In summary then, the church labyrinths, which made the circular unicursal design familiar to many thousands of medieval people, had several complementary functions and meanings, any or all of which might be understood in any single example. They bestowed honor and fame on human architects of genius and founding bishops of vision by implicitly comparing them to Daedalus. They affirmed the superiority of Christian art to pagan craft. As a setting for paschal dances, they encouraged the reenactment of the central events of Christian time: Christ's harrowing of hell and resurrection. They taught the similarities and differences between God's cosmos and man's world, between God's vision and man's, and asserted forcefully if ambiguously that what may seem chaotic to man's limited perspective is really perfect though complex order, part of the divine plan of salvation."

♦ ♦ ♦ ♦ ♦

Through the Labyrinth: Designs and Meanings Over 5,000 Years
Hermann Kern
Prestel, Munich, 2000 – ISBN: 3-7913-2144-7

[Note: This long stood as the greatest compendium of labyrinth knowledge. When written in 1982, it contained every reference to labyrinths in all of history, to the extent that the author could find them. Jeff Saward and I were co-editors of the English translation of this book. Alas, it is now out of print, which is a great tragedy and loss to the labyrinth community.]

"All pavement labyrinths with different layouts also have 11 circuits, as do the labyrinths in most medieval manuscripts. This is not the result of chance but of the observance of Christian number symbolism. In the Middle Ages, the number 11 was thought to signify sin, violation, excessiveness – since it exceeds the number of commandments – and incompleteness, since it falls short of the number of apostles, 12."

"From a theological point of view, the symbolic significance of superimposing a cross on the labyrinth is readily apparent: it is the symbol of salvation leaving its mark on the world of sin, dividing the world into a manageable cosmos of quadrants."

"Together, these aspects – west, death, entrance (initiation), 11 circuits – form the basis for a further interpretation: the act of tracing the labyrinthine path was thought to purify the Christian soul, to prepare it for meeting its Maker."

"The path leading out of the labyrinth must be understood as redemption. Christ, who is identified with Theseus, who conquers the labyrinth's ruler, the Minotaur, i.e., Satan, at the center, leads the way. . . . In Lucca, the labyrinth is located opposite an illustration of the Fall of Man, suggesting that it represented the way back out of sin into a state of grace."

"The immutable, unambiguous nature of the Christian doctrine of salvation shows the way out of the labyrinth. This is one of the reasons why all medieval Christian labyrinths are necessarily unicursal and do not encompass dead ends or choices . . .."

"In reference to Chartres, Batschelet-Massini gives evidence of a labyrinth dance having been performed by clerics during the Easter vespers, which celebrated 'the victorious resurrection of Christ and the second, completed creation of the world, this time in harmony.'"

◆ ◆ ◆ ◆ ◆

I wish to thank the authors and publishers of the books from which we have quoted not only for their permission to use the quotations in this booklet, but for their friendship and their contributions to the understanding and use of labyrinths. Each book is unique in its approach and comments, ever broadening the scope and use of labyrinths.

Robert Ferré
(*June, 2001*)

Appendix II

More reading for the 2013 Edition.

It is a slippery slope for me to begin to add more books or references. Where do I stop? As I write this, I'm sitting in my home office in San Antonio, surrounded by four bookcases filled with relevant books. As this is Easter week, I can mention books of sermons and meditations which borrow the labyrinth as a metaphor for organizing the text.

◆ ◆ ◆ ◆ ◆

The Lenten Labyrinth
Edward M. Hays

A Labyrinth Year: Walking the Seasons of the Church
Richard Kautz.

Neither of these is really about labyrinths, although they are alluded to and mentioned briefly.

◆ ◆ ◆ ◆ ◆

The Sacred Path Companion: A Guide to Walking the Labyrinth to Heal and Transform
The Rev. Dr. Lauren Artress

Dr. Artress has another book of interest, especially for facilitators. It is like a workbook to accompany *A Sacred Path*.

◆ ◆ ◆ ◆ ◆

The Forgiveness Labyrinth
Dr. William H. Senyard

Searching Amazon.com, I noticed a book that utilizes the labyrinth in a forgiveness process. The author is a pastor in the Denver area. I mention it here because of its use in churches. I only read the kindle sample. His style is extremely verbose and redundant, causing me to give up on the book. The topic, however, has great potential.

The Maze and the Warrior: Symbols in Architecture, Theology, and Music
Dr. Craig Wright

Dr. Wright pushes a lot of my buttons. He ignores the growing convention of calling unicursal patterns labyrinths, referring to them throughout his book as mazes (hence the title). Further, some of his comments and opinions about Chartres Cathedral are far off target, especially regarding the construction of the labyrinth. He is a musicologist, and therein lies his strength. The music he discusses from the medieval period would all have been ecclesiastic in nature.

Books on Chartres Cathedral

I have included in this book information about Chartres Cathedral as well as labyrinths. The labyrinth in Chartres remains the top design chosen by most churches for their own labyrinth. I feel that understanding the cathedral aids in understanding the setting and historical context of the labyrinth. For those readers desiring additional reading, I would like to steer you away from the books filled with speculation and silly theories (such as Templars building Gothic cathedrals). What really happened in Chartres is far more inspiring than the limited imaginings of modern minds. Here is my short reading list for Chartres Cathedral, in no particular order. There are, of course, many more books after these.

Mont-Saint-Michel and Chartres
Henry Adams

No list would be complete without this early 20th-century classic. It is so erudite than I only grasp a few of the references. It describes the two greatest religious monuments in France, not as a tourist guide, but as an analysis of the culture that spawned them. Adams, describing his own book, says that Chartres "expressed an intensity of conviction never again reached by any passion, whether of religion, of loyalty, of patriotism, or of wealth . . .. I wanted to show the intensity of the vital energy of a given time, and of course that intensity had to be stated in its two highest terms—religion and art." The social forces that led to the construction of great cathedrals has always fascinated me. Adams calls it "the point in history when man held the highest idea of himself as a unit in a unified universe." This is in fact the concept that led to the great height and openness of Chartres. Stones weren't just piled one on top of the other, as the Romans did in their aqueducts, requiring massive (and limiting) size and weight. Through vaulted arches and flying buttresses stone was used in a dynamic balance in which all elements work together. Thus were the historic limitations of stone superseded, with each element of the structure working in harmony with the whole, as if they, too, were units in a unified universe.

◆ ◆ ◆ ◆ ◆

Chartres and the Birth of the Cathedral
Titus Burckhardt

Titus Burckhardt knew western languages, Arabic, and Sanscrit. He spent a lifetime relating East to West, and expressing sacred symbols and principles. In a new 2010 edition, this work, translated from the German, has two forewords, one by John James and the other Keith Critchlow—both masters of sacred geometry. Burckhardt not only puts together far reaching elements of disparate cultures, he has a message. I recommend two more of his books, *Mirror of the Intellect: Essays on Traditional Science and Sacred Art*, and *The Essential Titus Burckhardt: Reflections on Sacred Art, Faiths, and Civilizations.*

◆ ◆ ◆ ◆ ◆

Chartres: The Masons who built a Legend
John James

In the 1970's, John James spent five or six years studying Chartres Cathedral stone by stone, coming to know the masons by their distinct templates, the size of the stones they used, the expertise of their work, and other clues. In his larger work (three volumes in French, two volumes in English), he has provided detailed drawings and descriptions of the cathedral which have revolutionized our understand of Gothic construction. This volume tells the story of the building of Chartres Cathedral for the lay reader. Now in his eighties, James is producing a 10-volume study depicting 1,500 Gothic structures in the Paris Basin, a summary of his life's work. He lives on 240 acres in the Blue Mountains in Australia, completely off the grid (solar, propane, wood). There he has a retreat center called The Crucible where he and his wife Hilary practice transpersonal psychology. Their work is captured in his book *The Great Field: Soul at Play in a Conscious Universe*. See his website: www.johnjames.com.au.

◆ ◆ ◆ ◆ ◆

Universe of Stone: A Biography of Chartres Cathedral
Philip Ball

Ball has written ten erudite books on science and nature. What makes this book on Chartres so powerful is that he "gets" it. He describes not just what was built, as John James has done, but why. I have always felt that the twelfth and twentieth centuries hold much in common: world-changing inventions, travel in a shrinking world, scientific investigation, massive social change, economic opportunity. In Chartres, when you look at the stained glass windows, the characters look like cartoon figures. Is that because they could build a whole cathedral but couldn't draw people? Of course not. Ball explains this very well.

"The significance of objects and events was determined not by those things in themselves but by what they represented. This is clear in medieval art, the non-naturalism of which says less about any deficiencies in the technical abilities of the artists than about the way they conceptualized their experiences. They could see of course that skies were not made of burnished gold, that babies were not proportioned like adults, that people's faces were not all identical. But it did not matter what they saw. They aimed to depict the underlying nature and structure of a universe that, in the here and now, was transient and imperfect.... It would not be stretching the point too far to say that this art was performing a function that science aims to fulfill today: to simplify the world, to strip away what is contingent from what is essential, to reveal the framework. Art existed to reveal the deep design of God's creation."

◆ ◆ ◆ ◆ ◆

Chartres: The Making of a Miracle
Colin Ward

I forgot I owned this book until looking through the bookcase for books to list here. The underlining shows I read it, however long ago. There are many scholarly works about Chartres Cathedral. This one stands out because it is short, less than 100 pages, concise and to the point.

◆ ◆ ◆ ◆ ◆

Bread, Wine, & Money: The Windows of the Trades at Chartres Cathedral
Jane Welch Williams

The windows in Chartres Cathedral are unique in that the lower registers depict forty-two artisan trades. Virtually every guide to the Cathedral will tell you that these represent the guilds that donated the windows. Jane Welch Williams has a completely different theory. In supporting it, she provides the best history of the city of Chartres and its social dynamics that I have read anywhere. Most surprising is the tension between the church and the town itself, which even led to riots. Under such conditions, why would the guilds then contribute money to the church? Williams suggests that they didn't, presenting a different idea of what the windows represent.

Chartres Cathedral: Image of the Heavenly Jerusalem
Anne Prache

I once wrote to Anne Prache, asking her to address one of the groups I took to Chartres. By then she was elderly, having long retired from her position at the Sorbonne. She declined. This very hard to find book gives meaning to the art and architecture of the cathedral. How many times have you read that walking the Chartres labyrinth was a surrogate pilgrimage for going to the Holy Land to visit Jerusalem? This misunderstanding comes from literature calling the labyrinth the road to Jerusalem. The Jerusalem it refers to is heaven, the celestial Jerusalem, not a city in the Middle East. Chartres represents God's home on earth. Prache describes it all very well.

◆ ◆ ◆ ◆ ◆

Whew! Wasn't that fun. I can go on about this topic for hours. Better for you to read the books yourself.

Robert Ferré
(April, 2013)

12 Reasons to Have a Church Labyrinth

This list first appeared on my website:
www.labyrinth-enterprises.com/12reasons.html
Here is its latest version. There are, of course, many more than
twelve reasons for a church to have a labyrinth.

1. The Labyrinth Updates Spirituality

Churches are constantly in a state of transition as they attempt to remain relevant to society. The Reverend Dr. Lauren Artress has stated, "The movement in the church to reclaim its lost spiritual tradition is enormously significant."

The labyrinth is an ideal spiritual tool which can be used to reach people who don't relate to the church as an institution. The labyrinth is personal, generic, and meaningful. It also helps to build community. While providing labyrinths is a wonderful public service to the community, it can also be a form of outreach for the church. I know of many instances in which people became involved in churches as members and participants after first coming to walk the labyrinth.

The labyrinth, then, can be used to draw new people to a church. Whether they like what they find, and whether they decide to become involved in the church, is beyond the capability of the labyrinth. That depends on the church and what it has to offer. The labyrinth enhances the image of being progressive, of incorporating new elements.

One of the ways this has been done in many places is to combine labyrinth walking with Taizé music. Taizé is an ecumenical community in France which desires to unify the divisions and differences that separate the Christian family. As a result, they have no dogma to teach, since dogma divides rather than unifies. Their services are comprised almost entirely of repetitively singing beautiful chants, in

Latin or a variety of languages. Labyrinths also have no dogma, "speak" many languages, and unify.

2. The Labyrinth Is Traditional

The labyrinth goes back 5,000 years or more. Beginning as early as the fourth century CE, Christianity adopted the labyrinth as a symbol, changing the design to imbue it with specifically Christian meaning. For almost a thousand years there has been an identifiable Christian labyrinth tradition. This movement reached its peak at Chartres Cathedral, in France, with the installation of an elegant labyrinth into the nave floor in 1201 during the construction of the magnificent new Gothic structure.

The labyrinth incorporates many levels of symbolism within its sacred geometry. Its circularity and concentric circles reflect the cosmos, atoms, and DNA. The geometry comprises the very principles of manifestation utilized by the Divine Hand in its creation of the physical universe. The labyrinth is an archetype, which reflects the nature of human experience.

In our modern world we have lost touch with our origins, our roots, even our true identity. The labyrinth is the bridge that connects us to these things, to a long-forgotten part of ourselves. That's why it touches people very deeply, often in a way they can't verbalize, as the context itself is ancient.

3. The Labyrinth Is Contemporary

There is scant record of how the labyrinth was originally used, other than for rituals during Easter. Therefore, a new format has been adopted, to serve our modern needs. Whereas today the labyrinth is democratic, and available to anyone who would walk it, in the past it may have been reserved for ritual use by the clergy only.

Walking a Sacred Path: Rediscovering the Labyrinth as a Spiritual Tool, by Lauren Artress, has been helpful in suggesting ways to make the labyrinth relevant. Borrowing three steps described in the early

Middle Ages, she applies them to the stages of walking the labyrinth. They are:

1. Purgation: Releasing and shedding as we walk towards the center
2. Illumination: Resting in the center to receive inspiration
3. Union: Returning to our lives with a new awareness

Lauren Artress writes, "The labyrinth is truly a tool for our times. It can help us find our way through the bewildering multiplicity, to the unity of source. The labyrinth is an evocative experience. The labyrinth provides the sacred space where the inner and outer worlds can commune, where the thinking mind and imaginative heart can flow together. It can provide a space to listen to our inner voice of wisdom and come to grips with our role in humankind's next evolutionary step."

Carole Ann Camp, co-author of *Labyrinths From the Outside In: Walking to Spiritual Insight, A Beginner's Guide*, expands the process to seven steps:

1. Preparation
2. Invocation
3. Going in
4. Staying in the center
5. Returning to the world
6. Thanksgiving
7. Reflection

Camp's co-author, Donna Schaper, writes, "One of the key reasons people walk labyrinths today is to have the experience of the simultaneity of past and present. In walking the labyrinth we link with other cultures and eras. We also link body and soul; we simultaneously have a physical and spiritual experience. We make metaphors work for us. The journey is one foot after another, and it is a path to the holy place inside us."

Schaper discusses the ecumenical, postdenominational environment of churches today. The labyrinth fits right into that picture. It is at the same time ancient and modern.

4. Labyrinth Walking Is a Spiritual Practice

Spirituality requires attention, hence the necessity for spiritual practice. Walking a labyrinth is such a practice. In this way, the labyrinth makes spirituality accessible to everyone. It is a form of personal meditation and devotion, not a piety of obedience.

The labyrinth goes beyond our limited, conditioned personality and learning, tasking us to a deeper place of awareness and revelation. In that state, we can practice being in the presence of God. We can sing, pray, or dance. While walking the labyrinth we can repeat a phrase as our mantra, such as "Lead me," or "Be still and know I am God." In the Old Testament, David advised Solomon to "Walk in the ways of God."

Lauren Artress was worried when she first began using labyrinths. It was clear that they were powerful, but to what end? Could labyrinths be too much? Could they overwhelm? Could they injure people? She reports, "After months of walking the labyrinth and listening to the experiences of others, I began to trust the labyrinth." She goes on to describe developing faith in the process, which I take to be the same as trusting the spiritual practice.

When teaching people how to walk the labyrinth, I try not to create unreasonable expectations of what will happen. I believe that the labyrinth meets each person where they are and helps them to take the next step on their spiritual path. Because it is so personal, it is a spiritual practice accessible to everyone.

The labyrinth is a spiritual tool. We learn how to use tools expertly through practice. They become extensions of our own abilities, allowing us to be stronger or faster or more accurate. In the case of the labyrinth, it helps us to meditate more profoundly, and to go deeper within. With practice comes improvement. Therefore, walking a labyrinth is best done on a consistent basis to obtain the maximum results.

5. The Labyrinth Embodies Prayer

As a form of body prayer, the labyrinth embodies our experience, keeping it from being just theoretical or mental. Someone said that bodies can synthesize what the head can only distinguish. Saint Augustine is often quoted as having said, "It is solved by walking." Labyrinth walking has been called the laying on of feet.

One of the most noticeable effects of walking the labyrinth is stress reduction. We can see the difference in our physical bodies. Stress kills, and the reduction of stress heals. The same is true with balance. Our priorities get far out of kilter sometimes. When that happens, we experience dis-ease. The labyrinth brings us back to a state of equilibrium. It can contribute to bodily healing and well-being. Being physical, the labyrinth is anchored in time and space, just as we are.

Any labyrinth maker can describe how important are the physical traits of the labyrinth, namely its size, location, and orientation. Outside of the Christian tradition are other labyrinth traditions, one of which utilizes dowsing. Rather than dowsing for water, one dowses for the features of the labyrinth. This approach concludes that it is the physical properties of the labyrinth that generate power. Thus, the mechanical details are important. The Christian tradition, on the other hand, sees the power coming not from the labyrinth, but from the act of walking. Thus, it is we who energize the labyrinth, not the other way around. Both of these traditions are credible. In Christian labyrinths, however, more importance is usually given to the symbolic than the physical properties. It is the physical nature of our involvement, using our whole bodies and our senses, which is most important.

6. The Labyrinth Is a Form of Pilgrimage

Pilgrimage is an outer journey with an inner purpose. It takes us away from the routine of daily life to sacred places where the veil seems thinner and spirituality more approachable. The labyrinth does this. It organizes our experience and engages us in spiritual

67

travel. Some call it a quest. In the labyrinth we walk in a way we don't walk elsewhere, which leads to a new kind of experience.

Pilgrimage is a tradition in most religions, from walking in processions in Lourdes to circling the Kaaba in Mecca. Taking time out to honor one's relation to God is important and essential. Even today, thousands walk on pilgrimage to Santiago de Compostella, in Spain. Being on a spiritual journey is the perfect metaphor and image for both life and the labyrinth.

In Chartres Cathedral, one of the greatest of all Gothic cathedrals, our spiritual journey is symbolized everywhere – in the sacred geometry, the art, the architecture, and the labyrinth. The church is the gateway, the connection between heaven and earth. In the same way, the labyrinth is the threshold between the physical world and the metaphysical, between the outer and the inner.

While the labyrinth symbolizes the route, no one can take it for someone else. We must each find our own way. I particularly like the approach of the Taizé Community, which works with thousands of young people. The Taizé brothers tell them, "We don't have any answers to give you, but we will be with you and assist you to find your own answers." The labyrinth is the same, in that it imposes nothing, but allows each person to find that which is meaningful to them.

I once asked brother John at Taizé why they don't include some older adults in their group discussions with young people, as they have more life experience. "Because," he told me, "we can't keep them from teaching." The adults want to give them all the answers. The brothers want the young people to discover the answers on their own. No one else can take your journey for you.

Life can be many kinds of journeys. The world has endless choices and paths, most of which lead nowhere. The labyrinth path is sure, certain, dependable. It is an appropriate and accessible place to go on pilgrimage.

7. The Labyrinth Is a Spiritual Aid

Each of us may have to pursue his or her own individual spiritual quest, but that doesn't mean we don't need some help. Our success rate is vastly increased by the utilization of spiritual aids. In some instances, people engage a spiritual director or counselor to advise them. Likewise, the labyrinth can be a spiritual aid. According to Lauren Artress, "The labyrinth can play a significant role in the field of spiritual direction."

It's ironic, of course, that we actually find our way in the labyrinth, when it is commonly used as a literary metaphor for a place in which we get lost amidst confusion and complexity. Such literary devices are really referring to mazes, which have many paths and dead ends. In a maze, one loses oneself, whereas in a labyrinth, one finds oneself. Walking the labyrinth brings order to chaos.

It is much easier to drink water out of a container, such as a glass. The glass is only the aid, not the water, but it makes the water readily available. As with a glass, the labyrinth is a container. It is a road map, a menu. Drinking the water, taking the journey, or eating the meal is up to us. The labyrinth makes our spiritual quest possible through organizing us. Through its format and guidance, the labyrinth acts like a spiritual homing device, a compass and a gyroscope, all in one.

It is common for us to criticize and find fault with our spiritual efforts. We see ourselves as falling short of the mark. The labyrinth, with its single path, offers a way that is certain. That doesn't mean, however, that it is easy. In a labyrinth there are no short cuts. We must walk the entire length of the path. If we persevere, the outcome is assured.

The labyrinth is a source of spiritual self-esteem, a positive feedback loop. We go to the center of the labyrinth. In all books of symbolism the center stands for God, creation, truth, wholeness, healing. That is where the labyrinth leads us, and with those gifts, we return back to our lives.

With a hammer, we can build a house. The hammer is important and extremely helpful, but the objective is the house. The same is true with the labyrinth. We should not confuse the tool with the purpose. Unless we are just seeking exercise, our goal is not a labyrinth walk, but a spiritual experience. The labyrinth has shown itself to be a very efficient spiritual aid. Ultimately, of course, the result depends on the user. A physical tool only lends assistance. It makes no decisions.

8. Labyrinths Circumvent the Intellect

Every religious tradition has some ritual or technique to take us past our thinking mind. It is as if we have a crust on the outside, made of our personality, our learning and conditioning, cultural socialization, and intellectual activity. But there is much more to us, within. The labyrinth leads us deep within, to our center, where we encounter our authentic selves, far beyond the limits of the shallow mind.

In a society filled with noise pollution, words and images flood us from TV, radio, social media, and the Internet. It is overwhelming. Walking the labyrinth is a non-verbal experience. It helps to cultivate our inner life. Rumi, the Sufi poet, said that we should spend at least as much time in the invisible world as in the visible. In the same way, we can spend time in the non-rational, non-thinking, non-verbal world.

Pierre Teillard de Chardin wrote that truth cannot be found in the world. We must find it by going within. Once we find it, we realize that the truth is universal. The point where that which is most personal becomes All That Is, the universal, he called the Omega Point. Walking labyrinths, then, is not a selfish act, as the resulting truth will shine out into the world through our lives.

Lauren Artress writes, "To walk a sacred path is to discover our inner sacred space. . . . Walking the labyrinth clears the mind and gives insight into the spiritual journey." We can't think our way. We must trust forces greater than ourselves. When we go to our center, it is really The Center, the same center in which we shall all meet as One. It is the Divine.

9. Outdoor Labyrinths Add Another Dimension

Labyrinths help us to think outside the box (sanctuary). In 1996, a group of pilgrims led by Lauren Artress and myself walked labyrinths both in Chartres Cathedral and in a friend's garden in Germany. Some of the group found their experience on the garden labyrinth to be more powerful. One reason may well have been that the garden labyrinth was outdoors, on the ground, in a beautiful setting.

There is an attraction to outdoor activities, such as campfires and Easter sunrise services. Walking the labyrinth outdoors, one experiences a range of circumstances and weather, from hot to cold, dry or rainy, day or night. It has great variety, just like life.

There is a connection between nature and the labyrinth. In our modern society we have lost contact with the changing of the seasons, the constellations, the freshness of the air. Walking an outdoor labyrinth incorporates these aspects to enhance our experience.

Outdoor labyrinths can be used for other purposes. Chairs can be set up on them for Sunday school class, or a wedding may be held. Some of the outdoor labyrinths we build include a lectern or pulpit for holding outdoor services. The labyrinth could hold tables for refreshments, information, crafts booths, or a rummage sale. Making practical use of the outdoor labyrinth in no way diminishes its power as a spiritual tool.

Furthermore, outdoor labyrinths are usually available 24 hours a day, even when the church is locked.

10. Labyrinths Build Community

When walking the labyrinth with others, a joining takes place. Community is formed. On numerous occasions people have stated to me that they prefer to walk the labyrinth alone, and not be distracted by others. Later, after walking as part of a group, they expressed surprise at how poignant their experience was. The group energy helped to create a space which enhanced each individual experience.

The community built by the labyrinth extends beyond walking it together. The labyrinth committee, in overseeing and maintaining the labyrinth, works and trains together, introducing others to the labyrinth. Often the committee is involved in the planning, fundraising, and even construction of the labyrinth.

There is only one problem in the world, expressed in many variations: separation—from God and each other. The only solution is to join together, to move from one to One. The labyrinth challenges the image of life as a lonely, hazardous journey through a maze. It is much more enjoyable and fruitful to pursue this journey with others rather than in isolation.

One of the most common observations during the sharing time after a labyrinth walk is the realization that we are all on the same path, even if it looks like people are all going in many different directions. The people in the paths adjacent to the walker may be walking in the opposite direction. Even on a given path, some people are going in while others are coming out. Yet everyone is pursuing the same journey.

Donna Schaper writes, "The labyrinth lets people walk together and separately without agreeing on anything. The very ancient nature of the labyrinth combined with the archetypal metaphor of its design draws us to absolutes that transcend any human constructs that have separated humanity into arbitrary religious categories for centuries. That is why labyrinths are so welcome today: they allow each of us to find our own center in our own way."

11. Labyrinths Offer A Time to Listen

Certainly one of the great lessons in life is to give up being in charge, to get out of our own way, and to turn things over to guidance from a higher source. Author Jill Kimberly Hartwell Geoffrion has written several poetic books about using labyrinths. She has found that the labyrinth has many gifts for us, but to receive them, we must be receptive. We must listen. How else can we know if our supplications have been heard?

Walking the labyrinth is time out from our daily schedule. We aren't checking items off our list of things to do, or planning the menu for dinner. Walking in a labyrinth is a gift we give to ourselves. During the walk, we can relax our mind but we still must remain alert, to follow the path. This state of relaxed alertness is the ideal form of meditation. With our sense of awareness, we are open to any messages or inspiration or creativity that may come to us.

In one instance, a labyrinth walker received a clear urge to call her sister, from whom she had been estranged for more than ten years. That evening, when she made the call, her sister replied, "Just today I was thinking that we should resolve our differences. I'm so glad to hear from you."

When listening, we can learn. We can discover. While talking or demanding or lecturing or analyzing, we close ourselves off. Within listening there is an element of surrender that takes us out of time and space. Some call it Holy Listening.

Lauren Artress writes, "The labyrinth is a spiritual tool meant to awaken us to the deep rhythm that unities us to ourselves and to the light that calls from within."

After a labyrinth walk, during the sharing session, reflective listening is an essential tool for the facilitator. Even if someone has expressed a problem or difficulty or emotional vulnerability, the purpose of the sharing is not to fix or solve problems, only to be together and support. Reflective listening is a trained skill in which the person is assured that he or she has been heard.

12. The Labyrinth Addresses Our Deepest Needs

One researcher believes that labyrinths have reappeared throughout history at times of social upheaval and spiritual crisis. One can certainly argue that our world, and our society, are out of control. Decisions for policies that affect the public are made with political or commercial objectives in mind that don't serve us, especially with regard to our spiritual needs. Response to our inner longing is not likely to be found in our secular institutions. That's not their mandate.

Meeting such needs is the appropriate mission of churches. Labyrinths can help. Labyrinths restore the balance and the inner awareness that the world lacks. Of course, we, too, are the world, so eventually, the world itself changes as a reflection of our personal change.

Donna Schaper writes, "Walking the labyrinth is not about escaping into the center and leaving the world, it is about experiencing Spirit in the center so that you can live in the world in a more blessed way."

The labyrinth has been shown to be very effective in addressing grief. The labyrinth is feminine, embracing, nurturing – qualities that are in great demand. People often respond emotionally during a labyrinth walk without actually knowing why. They feel safe in its embrace. It gives people a chance to charge their batteries before going back into the fray.

Labyrinths have healing qualities on many levels, emotional, psychological, physical, spiritual. The labyrinth revival has come at a time when we greatly need healing. Healing must be an inside job, which is exactly how labyrinths function.

Why are labyrinths are undergoing a great revival? Because we need them.

Resources

GENERAL

www.labyrinth-enterprises.com
Our website is quite extensive, with free instructions and other articles of interest.

www.robertferre.com
This is my personal website. It has material other than labyrinths, including a blog on which you can ask questions—about labyrinths or other topics.

www.labyrinthsociety.com
I was instrumental in the founding of the Labyrinth Society at two meetings in St. Louis, MO, in 1997 and 1998. Now it is a thriving international organization with an annual gathering and many website resources.

www.labyrinthos.net
Jeff Saward, editor for more than 30 years of *Caerdroia*, a journal for labyrinths and mazes, is far away the world's greatest authority on labyrinths. He has authored excellent books on the subject, has the most extensive collection of labyrinth photos, and offers full consulting and construction services. His website is fascinating to read.

www.veriditas.org
Veriditas was the first and remains the leading source for training labyrinth facilitators. They sponsor events in Chartres, France, which can be life changing.

www.labyrinthresourcegroup.org
The best resource for labyrinths in schools, the Labyrinth Resource Group of Santa Fe has been doing this work for more than a decade.

FINGER LABYRINTHS

Finger labyrinths have the same benefits as walking labyrinths. Here are some sources for buying them:

www.paxworks.com
www.iSpiritual.com
www.relax4life.com

LABYRINTH BUILDERS

www.labyrinthsinstone.com
The site for Marty Kermeen, the world's greatest paver and stone labyrinth maker.

www.labyrinth-enterprises.com
We continue to offer a full range of design, consulting, and installation services.

www.paxworks.com
John Ridder, a long-time colleague, offers both permanent and canvas labyrinths.

www.pathsofpeace.com
Lisa Moriarty, former president of the Labyrinth Society, makes both permanent and canvas labyrinths.

www.srfoundation.com
Lea Goode-Harris, originator of the Santa Rosa labyrinth pattern.

www.goldenspirit.com
Chuck Hunner, my number one onsite construction manager, is now going on his own. He also makes fabulous custom made jewelry, some with labyrinths.

www.discoverlabyrinths.com
Lars Howletts, officially an apprentice learning my methods, makes wonderfully creative labyrinths out of found objects. He is an excellent professional photographer. His work, including both labyrinths and photos, is inspiring.

This 17th-century drawing shows people walking the labyrinth in Chartres Cathedral, France. Note, just above the labyrinth, the portrayal of the rood screen (jube), which was removed a century later and about which little is known. The cathedral did not have chairs until the late 1700's, which one rented.

Made in the USA
San Bernardino, CA
02 September 2016